THE BRITISH COLONIES

Borgo Press Books by S. Fowler Wright

Arresting Delia: An Inspector Cleveland Classic Crime Novel
The Attic Murder: An Inspector Combridge & Mr. Jellipot Classic Crime Novel
The Bell Street Murders: An Inspector Combridge & Mr. Jellipot Classic Crime Novel
Beyond the Rim: A Lost Race Fantasy
Black Widow: A Classic Crime Novel
The British Colonies: No Surrender to Nazi Germany!
The Capone Caper: Mr. Jellipot vs. the King of Crime: A Classic Crime Novel
Crime & Co.: An Inspector Cleveland Classic Crime Novel
Dawn: A Novel of Global Warming
Dead by Saturday: An Inspector Cleveland Classic Crime Novel
Dream; or, The Simian Maid: A Fantasy of Prehistory (Marguerite Cranleigh #1)
Elfwin: An Historical Novel of Anglo-Saxon Times
The End of the Mildew Gang: An Inspector Cauldron Classic Crime Novel (Mildew Gang #3)
Four Callers in Razor Street: An Inspector Combridge & Mr. Jellipot Classic Crime Novel
The Hanging of Constance Hillier: An Inspector Cleveland Classic Crime Novel
The Hidden Tribe: A Lost Race Fantasy
The Jordans Murder: An Inspector Combridge & Mr. Jellipot Classic Crime Novel
The King Against Anne Bickerton: A Classic Crime Novel
The Mildew Gang: An Inspector Cauldron Classic Crime Novel (Mildew Gang #1)
Murder in Bethnal Square: An Inspector Combridge & Mr. Jellipot Classic Crime Novel
The Police and the Public: Some Thoughts on the British System of Justice
Post-Mortem Evidence: An Inspector Combridge & Mr. Jellipot Classic Crime Novel
The Return of the Mildew Gang: An Inspector Cauldron Classic Crime Novel (Mildew Gang #2)
The Rissole Mystery: An Inspector Combridge & Mr. Jellipot Classic Crime Novel
The Screaming Lake: A Lost Race Fantasy
The Secret of the Screen: An Inspector Combridge & Mr. Jellipot Classic Crime Novel
Spiders' War: A Novel of the Far Future (Marguerite Cranleigh #3)
Three Witnesses: A Classic Crime Novel
Too Much for Mr. Jellipot: An Inspector Combridge & Mr. Jellipot Classic Crime Novel
The Vengeance of Gwa: A Fantasy of Prehistory (Marguerite Cranleigh #2)
Was Murder Done? A Classic Crime Novel
Who Murdered Reynard? A Classic Crime Novel
The Wills of Jane Kanwhistle: An Inspector Combridge & Mr. Jellipot Classic Crime Novel
With Cause Enough?: An Inspector Combridge & Mr. Jellipot Classic Crime Novel

THE BRITISH COLONIES

NO SURRENDER TO NAZI GERMANY!

by

S. FOWLER WRIGHT

THE BORGO PRESS

An Imprint of Wildside Press LLC

MMIX

CONTENTS

CHAPTER I.

MR. CHAMBERLAIN'S POLICY

"You may be assured that Germany will not cease to emphasise the colonial problem before her urgent and fully justified colonial demands are fulfilled."

—Field Marshal Göring,
German Colonial Year Book, 1939

Prime Minister Neville Chamberlain desires peace, as we all do. He aims, he says, to bring peace to the world, and no man could have a nobler ambition, or one which would have the support of more general or more fervent prayers.

He sees, as we all do, that the threat to the world's peace comes from certain states whose peoples, essentially as peace-loving as our own, have been subdued to the control of ruling cliques having predatory policies, by whom they have been organised and equipped for war.

The Reticence of the British Government

His policy of assuring peace is particularly directed to the placation of the present rulers of Germany, which he rightly regards as the most formidable and the most actively predatory of these militant states. He calls it a policy for the appeasement of "Europe," and to this end he is prepared—with some important qualifications—to revert to the *status quo ante bellum*; and, in particular, he has been credited–or perhaps discredited should be considered as an alternative word—with the intention of negotiating for the return of some or all of the colonies lost to Germany through her defeat in the War which ended twenty years ago. It is at least true that his government has, at various times, avoided any explicit statement that they would not be surrendered, which, if such a policy were not secretly being considered, had become urgently desirable, to avert the growth of false and dangerous hopes in the German mind.

It is true that, under formidable pressure, not only from the ranks of the opposition, but from many of its own supporters, the present Government gave, on December 7, 1938, a denial of such intention which was explicitly, categorically, and even emphatically phrased, and which, to anyone unfamiliar with the methods of political strategy, might seem to be sufficient and final.

A Doubtful Pledge

But a narrow examination of assurances which were the result of a prolonged Cabinet meeting, where they must have been very carefully worded, and consideration of the fact that they came from those who were repudiating, under pressure, that with which they had certainly been disposed to palter before, may lead to a less confident conclusion.

Mr. Malcolm MacDonald's actual words were these:

> I do not believe that there is today any section of opinion in this country which is disposed to hand over to any other country the care of any of the territories or peoples for, whose government we are responsible either as a colonial or as a mandatory Power.
>
> That view has been expressed this afternoon in every part of the House, and that is the view which is shared by His Majesty's Government.
>
> We are not discussing this matter, we are not considering it. It is not now an issue of practical politics.

The treacherous ambiguity of this statement, apart from its general tenor, which does not improve on close examination, is, as Mr. L. S. Amery was quick to perceive, in the "now" of its final sentence, which implies, at least, that it either had been, or would become, an issue of practical politics, or perhaps both.

At the best construction, it is an admission that the present Cabinet had contemplated the possibility of such a surrender before the voice of popular indignation had warned them that they could not sustain it; at the worst, it may, with equal logic, be taken to mean that they have put the idea aside until the British public shall be in a more placable or indifferent mood.

And if this latter interpretation be wrongly held, the responsibility must be entirely at Mr. MacDonald's door, for his statement was followed by a direct question from Mr. Amery as to the meaning which that "now" might be construed to bear, which he declined to answer; and that silence may be considered to have been more significant than any words which he had previously selected to speak.

It has been argued by those who have sought to minimise the importance of the word he used and the subsequent silence which he maintained that an ordinary political prudence will confine itself, in such pronouncements, to the present tense. It is an argument which rates the public intelligence as low as its memory is certainly short. Suppose the question had been whether it were proposed to present the Third Reich with an English county, would Mr. MacDonald have considered that "now" to be so necessary a word that he would not even discuss the possibility of its withdrawal? It is too clear that the possibilities of ultimate surrender had not left the minds of His Majesty's Government, and that, without previous consultation, he could not withdraw a word which he had been instructed to use.

Not to Be "Given Away"

There have, it is true, been assurances by other members of the Government, equally emphatic in tone, that no part of the British Empire, nor any mandated territory—it is a distinction without a difference, as we shall come to see—will, under any circumstances, be "given away." But again the assurance becomes, on close examination, less conclusive than it was doubtless intended to sound. For might it not be argued with sufficient plausibility that some future surrender will be a matter of barter rather than gift? And bargains with the Third Reich—even if portions of the British Empire were suitable counters with which to play—have so far been so entirely one-sided that barter and gift have become synonymous words, so far as either can be properly applied to that which is rudely demanded, and violently taken away.

Certainly, there is no thought on the German side of giving anything in exchange which is of solid value either to us or them. At most, it might be a formula of unreliable words, from a source which has broken several of such pledges before, and has kept none. The *Kölnische Zeitung* (November 9, 1938) has suggested that these huge territories, with all their populations and wealth, should be handed over to German exploitation as a "generous gesture...thus providing the *preliminary conditions* for co-operation with a completely peaceful Germany."

"Stolen Property"

Another German newspaper, even more directly reflecting the opinions of Herr Hitler's Government, recently described these colonies as "stolen property." The adjective is, of course, absurd, and indeed comically so when coming from a nation which was built upon a deliberate policy of predatory wars, and calls the conqueror of Abyssinia its ally; but its significance would be hard to miss. What gratitude is to be expected for the return of stolen property? Indeed, what gratitude would be due?

And the return of these territories to a Germany which is to become "completely peaceful" in consequence—with the obvious inference that she will otherwise be liable to provoke war—is to be made in the name of justice, and not of fear. Although it is to be observed that it is only the results of one war, as affecting one country, that justice is concerned to adjust in this radical manner. It is not proposed to return New York to Holland, nor even the Cape of Good Hope; nor Louisiana to France; nor the Philippine Islands to Spain. It may even be contemplated that world-appeasement will be reached without restoring Abyssinia to the Abyssinians, although it was lost to them in a more recent war. Justice in these matters does not appear to be exactly blind, but rather to have a bad squint.

Still, Mr. Chamberlain's Government has been, and still is, disposed to entertain this policy. They may be right. They may see further than most. They may be inspired by a better faith. They may be offering us more than a moment of present ease, with a harder fate to be faced on a later day. But one thing is certain. We are on a downhill road, so that every step we take makes it more difficult to return; and it is one on which we have already gone far.

The Destruction of Austria and Czechoslovakia

We have watched the destruction of Austria.

We have done more than watch, we have assisted at the destruction of Czechoslovakia, advising the victim to remain quiet as the knife entered her throat. We have even paltered with the sickening lie that the principles of self-determination controlled the event.

We cannot alter this now, if we would: and there are many of us to whom its consequences were not clear in advance, even if they are now.

It must, at least, be well to look this next question of the ex-German colonies in the face: to understand what it will involve, both to us and them.

On Feeding Tigers

There is one thing that is sure. If we surrender the colonies, we shall have the pleasure of hearing Germany purr like a fed tiger. She will assure us that it is the last meal she will ever ask. So far as she is concerned, we may anticipate peace for a considerable period, providing we cease to interfere in matters which, she will tell us, with her usual courtesy, are no business of ours.

More than that, if we are complaisant regarding Hong Kong, and a few other distant trifles, of which most of us hardly know the names, there may be peace for us through the whole world, both next year and the year beyond. We are a rich empire. If the need arise, we can feed more tigers than one.

For those of us who love peace, it has the sound of a most pleasant dream. But to what manner of world shall we wake on the next day?

It is a question reasonably to be asked; and, if at all, it should be asked now.

Too Late for Regret

It is not merely that, if we surrender these colonies, it will afterwards be too late for regret. If we allow the issue to drift, as we are now doing, until the German people have become inflamed with expectation, it may be too late to decline without facing a war in which our allies would be fewer than might have been on an occasion which has now gone.

There was a day on which Austria might have been saved; but we let it pass.

There was a day shortly following the rape of Austria on which Czechoslovakia might have been saved. It is gone now.

We did nothing then; and when we began to bleat sympathy, it may have been too late for anything but war to have saved her from the invasion which she endured.

But let us not deceive ourselves as to what occurred. Herr Hitler, entering Krumau, boasted that he had come to a "reconquered" land, which he had won by merely baring a bloodless sword. He said nothing about equity or good-will, for truth has an obtrusive quality; and our aversion from calling what had occurred by the right word is a shame he sees no reason to share, and not much to pretend.

Methods of Butchering

But *before* the rape of Czechoslovakia he was disposed to describe what he intended to do by a smoother word; and *before* the colonies are surrendered to him he will be equally willing to talk about friendship, justice, and peace. If you can coax a pig through the slaughter-house door by scratching its back, is it not a natural thing to do? But after the door is locked on the inside, there will be a different scene.

A directly official statement issued (October 23, 1938) from the German Foreign Office in Berlin says that "a healthy sense of right" demands the return of colonies which were "wrongfully taken." If that contention be true, then their return is a matter of equity, which no other consideration should cause us to disregard.

But is it so? Is there a special dispensation for Germany, or is it a Nazi doctrine that *all* spoils of war should be periodically returned? Or perhaps she has come to see that they should never be taken at all?

A Change of Heart?

If so, she has had an extreme change of heart since she imposed the Treaty of Brest-Litovsk on a conquered foe, and, in that case, her sincerity would have been admirably demonstrated by inviting Europe to consider how the severities of the treaty could be undone.

She would say that it is impossible now. Too much has altered since then. So it has. The injustices of one generation cannot be put right by the next. The past is dead. If

15

inequities of any kind exist today, let the whole world unite to adjust them now, but they cannot be assessed by appeal to the conditions of other days. We must look at things as they are.

On these lines it is possible that Germany might advance an argument which has a more plausible sound. She might say: "Forget the past, if you will. But is it present justice that other nations should have great colonial empires, while I have none? Is it the way of peace to let such conditions endure?"

An Argument to Be Faced

This is an argument which has to be fairly faced, to whatever conclusion it may lead us; and in seeking its answer we may have to consider how both our colonies and those of Germany were acquired, what they have been to us, and most particularly what they now are.

We may also have to ask what, if any, disadvantages, military, political, or economic, Germany may suffer through having no such possessions.

But there is one thing to be first observed, if we have the courage to look at this question with honest impartial eyes. Such claims, such arguments, bad or good, may not be applicable to Germany alone. If present equity be the argument, then other European countries may urge that they have no colonial possessions approximating in extent or value to their own populations, or even to the relative number of the emigrants whom they send abroad.

A strict equity would give Poland a clearer claim than even Germany would be able to urge. Suppose Poland were to contend that, owing to her dismembered servitude during the nineteenth century, she had lost her opportunity of sharing in the scramble for colonial possessions which took place during that period, and that, now that her integrity is restored, she is entitled to expect that other nations, as an elementary equity, will adjust this difference? Should not France be expected to give her some part of her North African Empire, and England, being more richly endowed, perhaps Jamaica and New South Wales?

Should not Czechoslovakia, in contrast to the fate she has experienced, have been offered a portion of the Dutch East Indies, and the Belgian Congo been shared with Rumania, Sweden, Switzerland, and other comparatively uncolonied countries?

There might, even in a court of international equity, such as the world has not seen, be a negative answer, but it might be one which would apply to Germany equally. Let us consider first how our colonial empire came to be, and what it is today.

CHAPTER II.

HOW THE BRITISH EMPIRE GREW

The British Empire is, in some features, unlike any precedent organisation, racial, geographical, or political, within the limits of recorded history.

It is first observable that it was not made. It grew. It spread by an organic process; in which respect it is in vital contrast to the cardboard imitations which were deliberately cut out by other nations who have envied that which has been, and remains, antipathetic to their own genius.

Its nearest counterpart is the United States of America, which is not surprising, that great confederation having sprung from a most vigorous seed of the same tree.

It is a characteristic of our national temperament, which is commonly, and quite wrongly, attributed to hypocrisy by other nations who do not understand us—we cannot complain of that, often having difficulty in understanding ourselves—that we are rather ashamed than otherwise of an achievement, and a consequent world position, of which some would see occasion to boast.

We are particularly sensitive respecting the circumstances under which our ancestors entered upon and acquired these half-empty lands, and sometimes attribute to those bold-hearted pioneers degrees of moral turpitude which greatly exceed the facts.

The British Colonial Empire was not conquered by the military violences of a nation organised for aggression, as Germany certainly is today. Its acquisition was rather discouraged by successive Governments, lukewarm to its implications, and embarrassed by the problems it raised.

The Flag Followed Trade

Trade, the proverb says, follows the flag. So it may do. But it was rather the case with us that the flag followed trade. It was the enterprise of British merchants that gave us so many footholds in Asia; and the extension of rule in India resulted from war with French settlers and the changing alliances of its discordant factors, and gave the weak and mingled peoples of that huge peninsula a larger measure of freedom, higher standards of government, and a more settled peace than they had known from when Delhi looked up to a Turkish flag.

But was the English nation responsible or grateful for this? Warren Hastings was impeached on his return to England. So was Lord Clive.

Many colonies, including parts of South Africa, became ours as the by-products of European war.

Are Peace Treaties Lease Treaties Only?

If peace treaties can give no valid title to possession, the Cape should go back to Holland on the same day that

South-West Africa is returned to German. Or is there some mystic force in a demand that is made twenty years after the surrender has taken place? Is a colony taken from a defeated foe to be considered held on a twenty years' lease, becoming a permanent possession only if no demand be made at that time?

Other—and some of the most extensive and valuable—parts of our Overseas Empire were the fruits of hardy pioneering in empty lands, or of discoveries in uncharted seas.

Australia's Long-Empty Land

Australia lay in a desirable, almost vacant virginity for centuries during which it might have fallen to Japanese immigration, had the seamen of that nation been bold and searching enough to enter its lonely seas.

A virile island race, which, though not indifferent to comfort, preferred to worship at the altars of nobler gods, and which had not been taught to contemn the value of its own sons, did not only seek to market its goods wherever those could be found who would barter or buy, but sent out cargoes of living men to populate these distant, desolate lands.

The history of British colonisation—which has paused during our generation, though all those who have faith in our race, and its ideals, or desire that it shall have the strength in future days on which not only its security but its peace must finally depend, will pray that it may resume—included many noble and generous episodes, and others that deserve blame, which they have not failed to receive in our own tongue.

Pioneering Records

There are rough pioneering records of those who did not stint their own blood, nor, under provocation, to shed that of others. They commonly endured a two-fold struggle against the savage nomads of half-vacant lands, and the indifference or hostility of Home Governments, which would not give them support.

They are imperfect records of human heroisms, failures or faults, which are eternally unchangeable now. What was wrong we should not aim to condone. But it might be difficult to find, in the whole long confused record of British Colonisation, a parallel to the cold-blooded plot by which the present Italian government prepared for the destruction of Abyssinia, years before the incident occurred which was made the cynical pretext for the quarrel it had resolved to pick.

It is futile to condemn or condone that which is past. Our ancestors have gone beyond any judgment of ours, and our responsibility is no more than to see that their sins or errors are not repeated—nor the fruits of the valour which was theirs, and the hardships they endured, thrown away by ignobler hands.

We have to consider what the British Empire is now; what we have done for these German colonies which we accepted as cadet members thereof; what valid claim, if any, Germany has upon them now; and what will happen, both to us and to them, if we cast them out from our own communities, to be retaken by her.

CHAPTER III.

HOW THE GERMAN COLONIES ORIGINATED

The German colonies were more recently and more deliberately acquired than those of other European nations, and in contrast to the virile, spontaneous spreading abroad of a people whose Governments acted in a spirit of indifference, or even timid restraint, the German Government was active for their acquisition, while its people were indifferent to or even ignorant of the exertion it made, not to guide or restrain a natural exodus of population, but to acquire territory which it had neither discovered nor colonised, by deliberate violence or bargain, for its own aggrandisement.

It came late on the scene because the German Empire is no more than a recent combination of a number of small separate states of Northern and Central Europe, which were (more or less) of the same language and the same blood; and even this amalgamation was not the spontaneous expression of any popular urge, but was the plotted policy of the Prussian Kingdom, and achieved by drawing them into united military adventures; to which end, wars were forced deliberately upon three peaceful neighbours, and William, King of Prussia, became William, Emperor of Germany, in 1871, amidst a Europe which had already paid a most heavy price in blood and tears for this assertion of German power.

Forty years later they made, as we know to our bitter cost, a determined effort to secure wider supremacy in Europe, which we materially assisted to foil. Now a German Government more ruthless, more predatory, than any which went before, demands that it shall be put back in the position from which it struck previously, if not more than that. And its offer, in substance, is that, if we surrender all it desires of us, it will leave us alone, providing we remain quiet while it plunders in other fields.

During the first forty years of the existence of the German Empire—between 1871 and 1914, to be exact—it acquired, mainly by aggressive pressure on its neighbours, substantial overseas territories, in which it did a very moderate amount of colonisation, and was so far from improving upon the precedents of its European neighbours that its attitude to the native races it encountered was far less paternal than that of England had become at that period, and less fraternal than that of France.

The Negotiations for Colonies

Its constant pressure upon the good nature and peace-seeking disposition of successive British Governments would have been even more productive, and would have intensified present problems proportionately, had it not failed, time after time, to recognise when the limit of concession had been reached, and lost all by excessive greed, or by making some proposal of secrecy, or of bad faith to a third party, such as the most complaisant British Foreign Secretary could not endure. But, even so, they remain, to all who study them, an almost incredible warning of the extent to which the English Foreign Office will surrender to persistent blackmailing pressure, or pleas for "good-natured" concessions, if the public be ignorant of, or indifferent to, the event.

The history of these negotiations is open to all who care to read it with impartial eyes.

South-West Africa

In the case of South-West Africa, it was admitted that England had a prior claim which could not be ignored, and—as will be seen when we come to a detailed consideration of that territory—it was only the hesitant reluctance of the Cape Government to assume responsibility, which, as far back as 1876, the native chiefs had petitioned to accept, that opened the way for the establishment of a German trading station upon the coast, and subsequently to a formal German annexation, in which the British Government acquiesced.

Subsequent German brutality led to the Herero war, which continued for two or three years, until that gallant native race, by battle, by brutal massacre, and by flight into other territories more mercifully administered, had lost *eighty percent* of its population.

If this be taken as an *ex parte* statement, let the Hereros—whose numbers have now doubled under a kindlier rule—speak for themselves. Ask them what their attitude would be to a German return.

The Negro View

It is easy for us to condemn our own treatment of the aboriginal races of Africa, and it may be a most salutary thing for us to do. But the native African is the best witness of this. He has suffered, and, with important qualifications, been dispossessed of a land that he loosely held. His opinion is something more than academic. He observes, he communicates with those of his own blood over vast territories differently administered. He experiences, and does not quickly forget.

He has seen much of British domination. (He has also seen such things as the Bechuanaland Protectorate, and the Basutoland administration, which would be outside Nazi imagination.) Of German rule he has seen less, but he might call it enough. Ask the natives of any part of British Africa whether they will be content to be transferred to a German control. Ask the Hereros, who have known both! And this control would not be that of the old German Empire, of the comparatively tolerant Bismarck regime. It would be that of the intolerable Nazi tyranny, intolerant of any freedom of faith or speech, even among those of its own blood. What would be its conception of native African rights? What its treatment of any who should not bend to its ruthless will?

Enlisting Africa

This thought brings another of an even more serious and more sombre kind. In all our wars, it has been a settled policy not to enlist or accept the services of the native African, unless for local operations against those of their own blood. There are fundamental reasons for this, and we have acted upon it very much to our own disadvantage on more than one occasion. When the Boers invaded Natal, the Zulus were resolved and eager to rise against them in the British cause, in which event the investment of Ladysmith would not have occurred, and there was the utmost difficulty in dissuading them from this course. In the Great War, the Basutos offered to raise regiments for active service, which were declined. (They then raised a sum of £50,000—very large for them—towards its cost, as a voluntary demonstration of loyalty to the Empire. If natives in any German territory showed a similar spirit, its record is not easily to be found.)

The Prospects of African War

But what will happen if the Nazis should act in a contrary spirit? If they should arm the natives of whatever territories they should occupy, and train them for war? Would it be possible to avoid taking the same course in whatever parts might remain British? And would not a new horror be added to the war which, sooner or later, would devastate the African continent? A war that would surely come, for anyone who can suppose that the Nazis, having once strongly established themselves there, would remain permanently at peace, must have a most sanguine mind. It would be more probable that the pretexts and occasions for future aggressive wars would be worked out in Berlin before the first regiment had sailed to make its goosestep in the "reconquered" lands.

This question of the acceptance of native Africans as comrades in arms might raise itself even earlier, if the South African Union should decline to acquiesce—as it would if it should prefer present danger to future ruin—in the British surrender of the territory which it now administers. Shall we say that the Hereros are not to take up arms for the freedom for which they fought so stubbornly once before? Shall we turn our guns upon them? It would become a question of the utmost gravity to decide whether it would be legitimate, or possible, to forbid them to take up arms against those who massacred them before.

CHAPTER IV.

THE CAPE FOR HOLLAND?

IT may have been taken as jest rather than serious argument when it was proposed that the Cape might be returned to the Dutch, as its earlier owners, who only lost it by naval defeat. But if we ask ourselves *why* that suggestion has an absurd sound, we shall find that it goes to the root of the argument for the return of the ex-German colonies, and shows that root to have a rotten core.

For the decisive reason which would prevent even the discussion of handing over the Cape of Good Hope to Holland is not that it belongs to Great Britain, but that *it belongs to its own people*; and if those people seriously desired to be governed from Amsterdam—or Berlin—it is certain that England would not fire single shot to obstruct the realisation of that curious ambition. But *unless* it should be desired by them, the whole power of the British Empire (forgetting that they have debated at times whether they are under a kindred obligation to us) would be exerted for the defence of their freedom.

Two Conceptions of Empire

That is the crucial difference between the Nazi conception of Empire and our own. We may not always have seen so clearly, though this conception is self-evolved. It has been learned from no other land. But our present is not our past. The Dominions and Colonies of the British Empire are free to work out their own destinies. Some are adult, and some still too young or feeble to stand alone. But the intention is the same for all.

And is it not an obligation of honour that the ex-German colonies shall be free to fulfil their own destinies in the same way? Give them to Germany tomorrow, and we know how much freedom there would be on the next day for all who would not crouch to the crack of the Nazi whip.

They have been accepted into a sisterhood of free nations, and, against their own wishes, and without fault on their sides, can they honourably be driven out?

The rape of Czechoslovakia was half Europe's shame. The shame of the surrender of the African colonies would lie at our single door.

CHAPTER V.

THE DESTRUCTION OF CZECHOSLOVAKIA

Our subject is not the destruction of Czechoslovakia, but it is impossible to weigh it justly without understanding the equities of that unhappy event, on which an intensive German propaganda has obscured the issues to many generous minds.

It has been a common argument, even in English newspapers of customary sobriety and intelligence, that what was done was right, though it was not done in the right way. They have said (as would be true) that British people could not be expected to fight to oppose the self-determination of some millions of Germans oppressed by a foreign rule, under which they had been placed by obtuse or malignant provisions of the Trianon Treaty.

Bold and reiterated assertion of this half—or rather quarter-truth—has secured its wide acceptance among those who are thoughtless or ill-informed, but how far is it divided from the realities of the position! How scanty is its cargo of historical fact!

When, in the history of the last thousand years, was any part of Bohemia German territory? When did even

Austria have any dominion there except by such right as the sword will give? When, even under the heel of foreign conquest, were the natural boundaries of Bohemia broken apart? Why are the Tyrolese Alps admitted by Herr Hitler to be a heaven-set boundary, although there are hundreds of thousands of Germans on their southern side under Italian rule, while the ancient mountain frontiers of Bohemia have no similar sanctity?

What precedent of history is there, what basis of logic, for the theory that if men of a foreign race be invited to settle in a neighbouring country (as the ancestors of the Sudeten Germans were a Czech king) their descendants have the right not merely to return at will to their own land, but to expel or enslave their hosts, in all districts of their adopted land, where they may have become the more numerous? It is an argument by which some parts of Germany should have been surrendered to German Jews! And is there no part of London which should raise the Italian flag?

How, if Germany were pleading for justice before the world, could she repudiate the treaty which she had signed with Czechoslovakia, and the solemn undertakings she had given to respect her territory so few months before?

Why if she had confidence in her own claim, and desired no more than equity would concede, did she ignore Czechoslovakia's broadcast plea that she would submit her case to arbitration, which is surely much to concede when one state demands a part of its neighbour's land?

Why, if Hitler's heart bleeds for oppressed minorities of Germans who dwell in so many European states, does he not propose reciprocal treaties by which they would be granted the precise amenities which are enjoyed by minorities under his own rule? He might find that signatures to such documents would not be hard to obtain!

Why, we may even ask, should not Czechoslovakia have stripped the Sudeten Germans of their property and expelled them, with as much right as Hitler had to treat Jews in that manner, whose ancestors had been settled in Germany longer than Germans had made homes in the Czechs' land?

The answer to this and some previous questions is, of course, that Czechoslovakia was a weaker state than Germany; for which reasons also it was seemly for Hitler and his colleagues to speak of Dr. Benes in terms of vulgar abuse; but it would have been a different matter if he had spoken of them (with far greater provocation) in the same style.

If the wolf say that the lamb muddied the stream the accused creature must expect to perish for that offence, and if he point out that he drank lower down, he must be killed for the insolence of his reply.

Mr. Chamberlain's First Visit

To recognise such obvious facts as these is not necessarily to condemn the efforts which Mr. Chamberlain unsuccessfully made to save the victim of aggression, and successfully to avoid war. His first visit to Germany may be described as a noble effort to avert a supreme catastrophe. It was approved by all who love peace sufficiently to value the most slender chance by which it may be honourably preserved.

Even the concessions which he then agreed to press upon the Czech Government are not beyond defence, if they were the best terms he could get; and especially if he took that flight with the ugly consciousness in his heart that his government had betrayed their country by assuring it of military preparations which they had not made. We may give his purpose high praise, and economy of condemnation to what he did.

The Second Visit

And for the conduct of his Godesberg visit there must be more confident praise. On that occasion Hitler let his teeth show. Mr. Chamberlain could not hear the proposals which were then made without realising that it was no liberation of oppressed Germans at which they aimed, but the destruction by Germany of a peaceful neighbour, which was to be accomplished either by threats or bloodshed. His reply that he would communicate the proposed terms without engaging himself for their acceptance was of unassailable propriety.

It gained a few days' delay, during which the attitude of France, whose honour was pledged to Czechoslovakia in a way in which that of England was not, could be ascertained.

Of Munich

Of the visit to Munich, and what was agreed there, it is more difficult to speak, for the whole of what occurred may not yet be known. On paper, something was gained.

Something even in fact—something of procedure, at least—though much less.

It is when we come to what happened after that: to the fact that the Munich terms were not kept: that after the Czechs had been persuaded to abandon their fortifications, and become helpless, the International Council of Ambassadors which was to be their protection abandoned them to German inroads which had no racial pretext for their support, and which even exceeded the Godesberg demand, that we feel that history will have no more to do than to apportion shame.

Betrayal—by Whom?

To obtain the majority which a decision would require, either the British or French Ambassador, or both, must have yielded to German bullying, and settled frontiers in favour of that country without regard to any principles of racial, economic, or geographical justice, or the instructions on which they were pledged to act.

There is no possible escape from this conclusion. The boundaries to which they agreed are enduring witness of that to which they gave consent, either on their own volition, or on such instructions from one or both of their governments as no man of honour would have consented to carry out.

When they had finished, there was no occasion for the plebiscites which had been agreed, for all the districts in question—including some in which the German population was not, and never had been, ten percent of the whole—were in possession of German troops.

It is a matter on which some public pronouncement should have been made, for, whatever England's position may have been previously, from the moment that the Czech army abandoned their country's defences on our advice, our honour was explicitly pledged, as one of those on whom they relied to fix the new boundaries, or to control the plebiscites which were to decide them.

We may not have failed. Our ambassador may have given a solitary vote for justice, and seen his French colleague support the German and Italian ambassadors in the iniquitous proposals which were, in some way, agreed. Or he may not. We have no right to conclude that. We have no right to conclude anything on a matter of such gravity without proof. But, where England's honour is so closely concerned, we had surely a right to know.

CHAPTER VI.

The Way of Peace?

Czechoslovakia is gone, but Mr. Chamberlain's memorandum of peace with Germany remains. And he expressed at that time the anticipation that he would be meeting Herr Hitler again, to make further bargains of appeasement with him, though more recently his tone may have been less hopeful, less assured, the subsequent actions of Germany having given him reasons for that.

The way of peace is attractive to all, but it is legitimate to ask what the nature of these bargains is likely to be.

The scoffing parody of the rather childish verse which Mr. Chamberlain quoted when starting for Munich:

> If at first you don't concede,
> Fly, fly, fly again,

may be unjust in its implications, but it has some sinister support in a remark; which Herr Hitler is said to have made at that time, to the effect that he wanted nothing from Britain beyond the ex-German colonies, and there need be no war about *that*.

It is a remark which may be taken in either of two ways; as may that of Herr Hitler in his speech of January 30, 1939:

> Germany has no territorial claims against England or France except colonies. But this question alone would not justify war.

They may mean that, while he asked politely and hoped to get, a refusal would not break the friendship so newly born.

Or they may be taken as a singularly impudent suggestion of a contrary kind. And this latter interpretation is, unfortunately, more in agreement with Herr Hitler's customary methods of negotiation, and the press agitation for the return of ex-German colonies—particularly in Africa—which has been organised in Berlin, and which is also most actively at work in this country. We have seen enough of German methods in the initiation of previous coups not to recognise the signs of approaching crisis here.

And this interpretation is unfortunately supported by another passage in the same speech (January 30, 1939), the plain meaning of which did not appear to be widely observed, but which was of the greater significance because the general tenor of the speech was considered to aim at the avoidance of any immediate provocation. He said:

> One thing or other will happen. Either property will be distributed on the basis of force, and force will revise distribution, or distribution will be based on right and reason,

and then it will be impossible for a few Powers forever to possess all the colonies.

That is an explicit statement, with an inescapable deduction. Either "right and reason" will hand over some parts of the earth's surface outside Germany to Nazi exploitation, or it will be taken by force.

Only the date at which agitation will be superseded by violence is left unsaid, and on that point there are two precedent agitations—those against Austria and Czechoslovakia—which are complete in their consequences, to be observed, and one—that of Italy for portions of the French Empire—where the same technique is commencing to operate.

These precedents give a particular importance to the intensive German propaganda which has already begun, not only in that country, but in some directions here also.

The Campaign of Suggestion

The campaign of suggestion in some sections of the British Press, specifically that which aims to influence ill-informed minds, is particularly ominous in its implications. It is not necessary to suppose that our national Press is influenced by Germany to lead to the conclusion that for some reason other than a spontaneous desire to impart considered wisdom to its readers' minds, inspired certain journalists to perpetrate quite recently this gem of inconsequence:

> We cannot argue that the Germans, with whom we have made a naval treaty and the

Munich Pact, are unsuitable to rule native races.

Accordingly, we have no longer any moral justification for withholding colonies from them.

It is the sort of argument which might be hurriedly written by a man suddenly instructed to prepare the minds of his readers for the return of colonies to Germany, and utterly unable to think of any reasonable argument in its support. It is to be hoped that readers of this sort of matter will use their judgment before coming to any hasty conclusion.

But no one, who is not entirely biased, could have produced such preposterous arguments upon a subject to which he had given independent consideration.

Why should our "moral justification for withholding" ex-German colonies depend solely upon their fitness to rule native races? And how can the question of that fitness be affected, even remotely, by a naval treaty or a Munich Pact?

Yet later, the same argument—if it can be dignified properly by such a name—is repeated and supplemented in a leading article in the same strain which would be amusing, if the subject were not so serious.

It commences with the accurate statement that Hitler demands the return of these colonies. It goes on to assert that in putting that demand forward, Hitler makes it indisputably clear that he would not back the demand by military force.

That is how the declarations of Herr Hitler are frequently interpreted to the very numerous readers of the national Press, many of whom must lack leisure or inclination to examine this problem for themselves, but whose collective opinions may have an important influence upon a decision of the gravest consequences.

It concludes with this argument, which would be more pernicious were it less transparently what it is, that the issue is a moral one, and either the Germans are entitled to the return of the colonies on the ground that they are now fit to govern the natives, or we must dispute that contention completely and destroy it utterly and unmistakably.

There is an almost complete disregard for facts in the assumption that the unfitness of the Germans to govern alien peoples is the sole question at issue; and most reasonable minds might agree that, however great that unfitness may be, it would be a particularly controversial—and offensive—reason to select for refusal when others are available.

Propaganda of such a misleading kind may not have any convincing force to English readers, but it may have influences in Germany of the utmost gravity. For though whether or not Herr Hitler would deliberately provoke war on this issue may be in doubt, there is much less that he would bluff—perhaps too far to retreat—if he should be misled as to the fortitude of our own attitude on this issue.

CHAPTER VII.

Burglary by Consent

And so it seems that Mr. Chamberlain's reward for assisting Herr Hitler to burgle his neighbour's house is to be a similar visit to his own; but that, he is assured, will be no occasion for summoning the police, as a friendly talk will agree in advance the items of the swag which are to be taken away; and, after its removal, he may be allowed to put a moderately good lock on the door, for such safeguarding of what remains as it may be possible to reach, or worthwhile to attempt. That is the position we have to face.

Mr. Chamberlain, with the high purpose of averting a war which would profoundly disturb European civilisation, has announced his aim to be "the appeasement of Europe." And Herr Hitler, and his loud-speaking colleagues, have announced theirs, which includes the return of all the colonies which they lost in the last war, and the gathering of all European people of German descent into a single state.

If all that can be smoothly arranged, it may be reasonable to suppose that Germany will not disturb peace so long as she may find ready obedience to any further conditions she may exact from neighbours of narrowed boundaries and diminished prestige. (Whether the remains of the British Empire would find peace in other directions is a different matter.) For, under suitable conditions, Herr Hitler believes in peace. We have his own word for that, and for what those conditions are:

Hitler's Pacifism

"The pacifist-humane idea," he says in *Mein Kampf,* "is quite a good one in cases where the man at the top has first thoroughly conquered and *subdued the world to the extent of making himself the sole master of it.* Thus, first the struggle, and then the Pacifism."

So, if we start down the road that Herr Hitler points, we cannot say that we have not been told where he expects it to end.

The Candidates for Appeasement

The appeasement of Europe has commenced already. Austria has been appeased. With Mr. Chamberlain's concurrence, Hitler has appeased Czechoslovakia. With a short interval for the appeasement of the ex-German colonies, the process, if it be so allowed, will doubtless continue in an equally efficient and satisfactory manner. This process, which Herr Hitler's own book describes so frankly, and to which he has so exactly adhered, will involve the appeasements, in different degrees, of Switzerland, Poland, Denmark, Belgium, Holland, Yugoslavia, Rumania, and Lithuania.

After that, strengthened by such good meals (during which his Italian friends will have been similarly occupied in appeasing France), he may feel equal to the appeasement of Alsace-Lorraine; and then of the Tyrol, to Mussolini's naive surprise.

But after the whole of Europe has been appeased, with this admirable German thoroughness, what will the strength of Germany be? What friendships will England have? Of what manner of peace will she be assured? It will not be the peace of the "strong man armed that keepeth his house." It will not even be the quiet peace of the grave.

Perhaps there may be an "incident" where the frontiers of British and German Africa meet. Such matters are not hard to arrange. And after that there will be the peace of shame; or desperate, far less equal war than we could be required to sustain today.

A European Conference

But Mr. Chamberlain has a better plan. He will not leave it to Herr Hitler to play his hand in his own way. He will work for a European Conference, so it is said.

It may be called a good plan. But it is sanguine anticipation that Hitler will assent, unless it be very firmly pressed, and not then unless moved by other influences than those of friendship for his Munich guests.

It would be too like a partnership of butchers (not that it would be exact to describe Mr. Chamberlain in that way. His part has rather been that of the butcher's assistant: his occupation to rope the victim, calling a conference of horned cattle, and demanding contribution of beef.

Such a conference would be too likely to lead to a combination of countries unimaginative enough to resent the mutilation of their geographical and economic integrities, even in so worthy a cause. And, in combination, they would be of a most formidable power. But Hitler will prefer that they shiver separately, hoping that it may not be their turn to be carved up for the next dish.

The Way of Peace

Peace is the common prayer of a world on which science is inflicting troubles enough without the added burden of war. We are all agreed about that. The question is whether it be the way of peace to allow Germany to advance to a yet more insolent power. Whether the sole hope of a tolerable peace may not be to meet her now with a firm and united front. A poor hope, perhaps. But perhaps also the only one. With the possible consequence of awaking a terrible war—or the alternative of a worse on a later day.

The allusions to Mr. Neville Chamberlain in this representation of the position are not inaccurate, but yet, without qualification or addition, might be unfair in their implications.

He is fighting for the peace of a threatened world, with a sincerity which even his enemies, whether at home or abroad, cannot deny.

To test the sincerity of the dictators, even at some generous risk, may have been no more than a gamble, yet it may have been well worth the attempt.

Against the bad faith which abused the terms of the Munich settlement, the intensification of Germany's military preparations, the monstrous persecutions of German Jews, he has opposed an attitude which has gradually hardened. It is evident that, if his courage and determination are not lessened, his confidence is reduced, as has been shown by his recent statement in the House of Commons that it will be useless to hold any Conference of Europe Powers unless they show previous evidence that it is in a Spirit of good will that they will come together.

And it is to be observed that the dictators of Europe are two, and that neither of them would be loyal to his present partner for half a minute if—it may be a slender if— he should think it to his country's interest to make an opposite alliance.

But let us see now just what are the ex-German colonies which have passed into British hands, and what their surrender would mean to their present inhabitants, and to us.

CHAPTER VIII.

TANGANYIKA

Taking Africa first, and avoiding present discussion of such ex-German colonies as did not fall to British hands, it may be convenient to give precedence to consideration of the Tanganyika territory, not necessarily as more important than South-West Africa, but as being that which appears to be most directly threatened and in the greater danger, because it has only the British Government to speak and decide on its behalf, and South-West Africa is under the direct protection of the Union Government, which has had the courage to say that it is not either to be given or bartered away.

Ideas from Italy

The German anticipation in regard to the realisation of its ambition in equatorial Africa is so confident that a school has already been established in Berlin for the training of young women in tropical cookery and medicine, and in the study of native African tongues, with direct reference to this territory, although there is an alternative proposed in the Italian press. A recent article in the *Popolo di Roma* stated as a known fact (which we are not obliged to believe) that the British Foreign Office is preparing an alternative plan, which would cede to Germany certain portions of equatorial Africa of which the writer professed to have detailed information, to which would be added territories on the north shore of the Gulf of Guinea, and in Angola. The fact that these lands belong to Belgium and Portugal presented no difficulty. They are to have no more right of decision than had Austria or Czechoslovakia; but they are to be treated with more show of justice, *at Britain's expense*. They are to be compensated by gifts of "British territory elsewhere"—there is a sufficient vagueness about that to rouse unrest in almost any part of the British Empire where confidence in the courage of our Government may have been shaken by recent events—or heavy payments of British gold!

Europeans in Africa

There is a vague idea among many people who are acquainted with the history of East Africa that it is inhabited by Negro races which were happy and free until they were brutally subdued by inroads of white settlers from Western Europe. The truth, confused and contradictory in detail, as the history of wide areas, many races, and long centuries must always be, is largely of an opposite kind.

The excellent harbours and particular products of Eastern Africa have invited settlement there in times of Greek, Carthaginian, Roman, Byzantine, Persian, and Arab ascendancies. In the seventh century, when the tide of

Mohammedanism swept over the Eastern world, it found and overcame settlements far down that coast which were inhabited by people of Persian and Arab blood, whose arbitrary authority spread far inland with the effect of a blighting curse. For their export trade was almost entirely in human life. The native African was as "free," and possessed the land as much, as might be said of the herds of North American bison while they were being destroyed by the rifles of human foes.

In Ancient Times

The coming of the Portuguese, from when in 1498 Vasco da Gama sailed round the Cape and entered Mombasa Bay, was fatal to the Mohammedan ascendancy in these regions. Eleven years later a Portuguese fleet destroyed at Diu the combined Arab and Egyptian naval power, giving to their own country for more than a century a scarcely challenged supremacy both inland and upon Indian Seas.

Early in the seventeenth century, the Portuguese at Mombasa were massacred by Arabs, and towards its close a three-year siege of the same place by the Imam of Muscat resulted in its capitulation, from which date the Portuguese position was more precariously held, and at more southerly ports, so that the Arab vice-royalty at Zanzibar became the governing authority over a wide inland area; and the atrocities committed under this regime during the eighteenth century, and, with some modifications, until the middle of the nineteenth, were of an appalling nature, both in their character and extent.

The Slave Trade

But during the last century British influence began to be increasingly felt, and, to the confusion of those who can find nothing but evil to say of their own race when it ventures into remote and unfriendly lands, it was like the coming of a humane dawn.

In 1822 British pressure upon the Sultan of Zanzibar secured a treaty under which he undertook to prohibit the sale of slaves to "Christians"—*i.e.*, to white men—or their export to Christian countries. This modified a trade which, at that time, we had no power to destroy (and with which Dean Inge might say we had no business to interfere).[1]

---

[1] I should be sorry to do injustice to this versatile character, so I give his actual words, taken from the *Evening Standard*, October 14, 1938: "We must reconcile ourselves to the fact that if peace is the first interest of Great Britain, as it certainly is, we cannot prevent things being done by other nations which we think iniquitous.

"We cannot police the world. To ride abroad redressing human wrongs may be all very well for Sir Lancelot; it only makes Don Quixote ridiculous. We are right to make our protests. But when we are snubbed for our pains it is no use to shake our fists and curse."

It might be difficult to find a passage by any comparable contemporary writer containing baser or more foolish words, but the reverend gentleman contradicts himself so frequently that it may be unfair to treat any single passage as indicative of a considered opinion.

This one would be less deliberately discreditable, both to its author and the newspaper that gave it publicity, had it not been followed (November 24, 1938) by another article in which Dean Inge instanced some alleged atrocities in Antigua and elsewhere more than two hundred years ago, and after exhibiting the random inexactitude which disgraces some present day British journalism by de-

But meanwhile explorers, British and others, had penetrated far inland, discovering among fertile uplands the great lakes and mountain ranges amidst which the sources of the Nile were finally mapped. In doing this they observed that the Negro population was in process of rapid extermination by the Arab slave-raiders, and, with wider knowledge, efforts intensified to put an end to that infamy.

The British Navy at Work

The British Navy became increasingly active, and the wholesale slave-trade was greatly diminished by its efforts, though, up to 1870, the slaves exported annually from Kilwa alone were computed at 32,000. It was three years later that British pressure secured the closing of slave-markets and the suppression of such traffic throughout these regions, since which date there has been no more than an illicit, relatively small, and dwindling trade.

---

scribing the seizures of Austrian and Czechoslovakian territories as "both perhaps justifiable in themselves, but executed in a very high-handed fashion," went on to argue that, as atrocities were perpetrated by men of English birth, we ought to exercise "a little more courtesy in criticising our neighbours."

If we share the guilt of these alleged Antiguan atrocities, so that we must speak with muted voices concerning German persecutions of Jews today, then by parity of grotesque reasoning, those persecutions are justifiable, for all Jews must share the guilt of the assassination of a German attaché.

And unless Dean Inge will admit some time limit (of more than two centuries) which will free us from this restriction, we are all committed to a "courteous" tolerance of evil-doing to the worlds end.

Through the whole of this period, Germany had no foothold whatever on the East African coast, Her sole connection therewith—so far as the subsequent German Empire can be identified with such an event—was a small and abortive effort at colonisation during the seventeenth century by the Brandenburg East India Company, which was almost eradicated by Dutch hostility, and finally liquidated in 1717 by a payment of 7,200 ducats from the Dutch Government to the Brandenburg Co., for which sum the Company resigned all claims to, and any property it still had on, the East African islands or coast.

Germany Enters Africa

It was not until 1884—the same year that Germany asserted a protectorate over South-West Africa—that the good-tempered complacency of the British Foreign Office, badgered continually for colonial rights by the German Government, with which it was anxious to live at peace, assented to the hoisting of the German flag at M'buzini, and five years after the German Government declared a protectorate over the whole Tanganyika territory.

The Policy of Appeasement Begins

Two years later, England entered into a very curious treaty, in which she gave Helgoland to Germany, and received less than nothing in return; its provisions merely ratified and defined the extent of the German occupation of land to which England had a far stronger right, and declared an English protectorate over the Zanzibar littoral, which already existed in fact, and which was not Germany's to give. The policy of appeasing Germany with gifts, for which we got little thanks, had already begun.

CHAPTER IX.

Germany Asked for More

The African territories which Germany held between 1884 and 1914—no more than thirty years in all—were of huge extent, and bore witness to the energy with which the Government of the German Empire, during the few years of its existence, had elbowed its way into the colonial field; but they were little compared to the areas of Africa which it had intrigued, or sulked, or bullied to get. Incidentally, these would have included the Seal and Penguin Islands, which it had represented as barren and worthless rocks, and which a complaisant British Government might have been soothed to grant, had not the Admiralty pointed out that they lay on a sea route which £100,000,000 of British commerce annually passed, and the Cape Government that they contained a harbour large enough to accommodate the whole German fleet, and that they *were* of no possible value to Germany except as a future menace to the security of the Dominion.

What Germany Would Have Taken

They were still smaller compared with the portion of Africa which Germany subsequently mapped out for herself as her fitting reward if she should have won the last war. It went completely across the continent, and would have given her huge recruiting reservoirs of men, and naval bases which would have enabled her to dominate both the Atlantic and Indian Oceans, besides constituting a "halfway house" to the South American continent, which she is certainly ambitious to reach, and already actively intriguing to control—or, at least, to do so for the last twenty years, as the time would now have come when she would have been handing them back to their previous owners, with a goodwill gift of all the "installations" she had constructed during that period! That being, by her code, the routine procedure for territory "wrongfully" taken from conquered foes.

It may not be a point of major importance, nor an argument needed where there are so many stronger ones in the same scale, but it is a fact that this, and other German colonies to which we shall come, were not surrendered by their mother country as the result of her European collapse. It had already passed into British possession, as the issue of local war, which the Tanganyika Germans had themselves commenced by invading Kenya in 1914.

The Invasion of Kenya

Had they been told then that, if they could have captured and retained Kenya, as they had hoped to do, Germany would give it back to Great Britain twenty years later, on the ground that it had been "wrongfully taken," or that it would be a "generous gesture," they would have smiled excusably at this interpretation of the verdict of war—war which they themselves commenced in East Africa, just as they did by crossing the Belgian frontier.

During the first year, the Tanganyika Germans more than held their own. They were a considerable military force, and they raised a native army of 12,000 men for their support. They were driven back from their first invasion of Kenya, but a counter-attack on Tanga, gallantly attempted with inadequate forces, was repulsed with nearly 800 casualties. During the next year, the Germans made more than one raid upon the Kenya railway, and though the *Winifred* destroyed their only gunboat on Lake Victoria, and British naval forces bombarded Dar-es-Salaam, and sunk the *Konigsberg* in the Rufigi River, that cruiser's guns were salvaged and became powerful batteries in the land engagements that followed.

Mojoro Captured

Early in 1918, General Smuts being in command of the British forces, the Lumi River was bridged, and the Germans manoeuvred out of a retreat of forest swamps which they had been fortifying since the war commenced; and from that time almost continuous and sometimes heavy fighting drove them out of successive positions until, on August 26, their headquarters at Mojoro were captured, and Dar es Salaam surrendered eight days later.

The Flight of the Germans

Desultory fighting against an enemy who took full advantage of country in which communications were hard to maintain continued until the end of the war, but, by that time, the remnant of the German forces had been pursued through Portuguese territory into Northern Rhodesia, where, at the armistice, they surrendered a mixed force of about 3,000 followers and 1,300 fighting men.

The armistice did no more than register a success which was already as much ours in East Africa as on the Franco-German front.

What Tanganyika Is

Tanganyika Territory alone is of an area of about 360,000 square miles. It is a tropical country, with a climate varying widely with its rising altitudes, but not, on the whole, very suitable for European settlement. Malaria and other tropical diseases are endemic, rains are heavy, and heat, at some altitudes, is extreme. There are highlands in the southwest where the soil is fertile and the climate good. During the German occupation, it attracted few settlers.

It has now been under British administration for twenty years, and has made great progress, only retarded during the last twelve months by paralysing uncertainty as to whether it may be allowed to fall back into German hands. This doubt may not be complimentary to England, but can we say it is undeserved? It could have been relieved, and much dangerous expectation checked, by one definite word from its Governor, which he was only recently allowed to speak, and which is still only half believed.

A glance at the present condition of the territory, and a summary of what has been done during the period of English control, will explain how terrible, for those who have trusted us, that uncertainty is.

Freedom of Religion

Dean Inge suggests that to be quixotic is to be absurd. If so, the absurdity of British administration has been extreme. We have taken nothing for ourselves. We have allowed no preference for British goods. We have taxed ourselves to expend upon the territory £6,000,000, in ways which are not directly productive, and with no clear prospect that it will be returned. We have granted absolute religious freedom, which applies equally to Christians of every sect, to Hindus, to Mohammedans, and to the peculiar deism of the Masai tribes. We have developed the cotton-growing potentialities of the territory, settling, for this purpose, about 25,000 Indians on the land.

Freedom of Trade

The imports of *manufactured* cotton goods were valued in 1936 at £648,576; but this is no benefit to the cotton mills of Lancashire. Under our self-denying administration, this trade is almost entirely in Japanese hands.

Apart from Government goods, Tanganyika purchases more from German and Dutch sources (combined) than from this country, the total of British imports being less than twenty-five percent of the whole.

Its principal export, both in bulk and value, is sisal fibre, but cotton now reaches a value of from half a million to a million pounds annually, which, when the doubt of the future is removed, may be very largely increased.

Coffee is extensively grown in the highland areas.

Gold was first discovered under British administration in 1921. In 1936 production had risen to an export total of £489,196.

Coal is known to exist in large quantities and other mineral resources, now undeveloped, are likely to prove of great value.

Free Entry to German Settlers

Since January, 1925, free entry has been granted to German settlers, and, in the eleven years following, 3,068 Germans entered the territory under this permission. The British still outnumber the Germans, if immigrants from the South African Union be included in the former category; but if this were not the case, it would be interesting to see whether the Germans would argue that the preponderance of these freely-admitted German immigrants would give their home country valid claim to sovereignty over the land.

The requirement of most governments is that immigrants shall either retain their own nationality, or loyally adopt that of the land they enter.

The new German theory appears to be that immigrants may both acquire rights in an adopted land, and retain their previous nationality and allegiance, until they become sufficiently numerous to enslave those who have so foolishly let them in.

Population

The population of Tanganyika at the end of 1936 was made up of: Europeans—8,926; Asiatics (including about 10,000 Goans and Arabs)—32,255; Native Africans—5,105,705.

A year earlier—the latest exact figures available—the European total had included 3,956 British and South African Union settlers, and 2,665 Germans. Since that date the Germans have probably increased relatively and absolutely, though still somewhat the smaller total; but it would be inexact to conclude that the whole of the German population is desirous of being ruled from Berlin, though with the example of what has befallen those Sudeten Germans who were loyal to Czechoslovakia before them, they may be reluctant to speak their minds. The native population consists of eighty-five principal and fifty-two smaller tribes. Among these, sixty are of the Bantu group, two are of Persian or Arabic origin, and most of the remainder are Masai, or other Nilotic tribes.

The majority of the Asiatics are British Indian subjects, who would naturally dislike being handed over to Nazi exploitation.

The Dread of Exploitation

It is in that thought of "exploitation" that the dread of people of every religion or race, including many Germans, in the territory lies.

Germany has everything already which can be hers, if nothing be taken away. Her nationals have entire trading freedom, entire religious freedom, entire freedom to settle upon the land in equality with other citizens. How can her position be improved, except at the sacrifice of economic advantages or personal freedoms which are at present enjoyed by all? What, it may further be asked, would any pledge she might give to respect present liberties or privileges be worth?

Even those of her own blood would be less secure. Among the twenty-three Christian Missions which are working in the country with complete equality now, there are those of several German Protestant sects which are not very popular with the Nazi Government. What would be their fate if they should dare to oppose the exploitation of the native population which would certainly follow German occupation?

And what would happen to the British settlers who might be slow in making the Nazi sign? Or to the Indian cotton growers, left to the mercy of that race arrogant rule?

Incidentally, there are two small portions of Tanganyika which are no longer under British control. Following its British occupation, claims for parts lying contiguous to Belgian and Portuguese territories were made by those governments, and, in each instance, our Foreign Office good-temperedly admitted the claim, and ceded the desired territory, as she admitted also a claim by Italy to land South of the Juba river. Italy might well commence the New Deal by handing back what she acquired thus to her German friends, to which we scarcely could, and certainly should not, object.

The present law in the High Courts is English. There are Native Courts which administer local justice under the Native Courts Ordinance of 1929, over which the Government has a final control.

Order is kept by a police force of 60 European officers and about 1,600 native police. There is a garrison of 1,000 men of the King's African Rifles. Beyond that, the territory has no military protection at all. A contented population, which includes over five million Africans, is kept in order without difficulty by about 2,500 men who are mostly natives.

How, and under what conditions, and to what result, could this territory be placed under the Nazi heel?

CHAPTER X.

SOUTH-WEST AFRICA

We now come to South-West Africa, a widely different country from Tanganyika, in a more temperate zone, but with an aridity which, for many centuries, caused it to be only thinly populated.

It is still a poor country, and much of it can only become fertile if it can be successfully irrigated, which is, at present, no more than a doubtful hope.

The Diamond Beds

It has great mineral potentialities, but the most interesting of its ascertained resources are the diamond beds which lie along the seashore for hundreds of miles south and north of the mouth of the Orange River. These, since their discovery in 1908, have produced stones, in years of favourable prices, to a value of some millions. Very much greater quantities could be obtained, but the mining has been restricted in recent years, according to the policy of the South African Diamond Board, and during the depressed years 1931-34 was almost entirely stopped. Prior to that, exports in twelve years had totalled about £26,000,000. And since 1934 there has been a substantial revival.

It is a comparatively trivial matter, when considered beside some of the major issues involved in such a surrender, but it is worth observing that the transfer of this territory to Germany would involve the possibility of ruinous overproduction, which the Diamond Board, in recent years, has made great sacrifices to avoid.

Diamonds, with some unimportant qualifications, are useless stones. Their value depends almost absolutely upon their scarcity. The industry has been increasingly embarrassed during the last twenty years by the number and richness of the new fields which have been discovered, and prices, particularly during the lean years that followed the American financial crisis of 1929, have only been sustained by rigid curtailment of production. The diamond beds of South-West Africa are controlled by the Government, and are not allowed to break the market, which, in other hands, they might easily do with the smaller stones.

A Pastoral Country

Apart from mining of various kinds, as yet mainly undeveloped, South-West Africa is almost entirely a pastoral country. Prior to 1884, when the Germans appeared on the scene, it was mainly occupied by more or less nomadic pastoral tribes, of which the more important were the Hereros in the east, and the Hottentots in the south.

The Ovambos in the north were also a numerous people, but the majority of them were in Portuguese territory, particularly until 1915, when a portion of the tribe migrated southward, having had difficulties with the Portuguese authorities, and preferring to come under British rule.

Petitions for British Control

A prolonged war between the Hereros and Hottentots, and other disturbances in Namaqualand, had caused the chiefs of the Hereros and other tribes to petition the Cape Government in 1878 to take over control, and appoint Resident Commissioners to keep peaceful order. The Cape Government despatched a Commission of Enquiry, which received formal orders of submission from numerous chiefs, but the report on the country was not very good, and the Cape Government shirked the responsibility and the possible cost involved. They did nothing; and unsettled conditions continued for the next eight years, while the German Government intrigued in London for permission to occupy the land.

In 1883 a Bremen trading company established a footing with some show of legality by giving a chief in Namaqualand a hundred guns, some powder and lead, and £200 in English money for 150 miles of land, and, as a correspondence which followed between London and the Cape showed that the Cape Government could not make up its mind to accept responsibility, the Germans were allowed to annex the whole territory, with the exception of a Brit-

THE BRITISH COLONIES, BY S. FOWLER WRIGHT

ish settlement already established at Walvis Bay, and the islands along the coast.

The German Occupation

The history of German occupation that followed was one of continual wars. Chiefs who would have welcomed the overlordship of a British authority, which they knew, from the examples of Basutoland and Bechuanaland, would have brought justice and peace, resented a German invasion for which they had not asked, which was conducted in a hostile spirit, and had less consideration for them. In 1893 there was war with the Hottentots. In 1896 with the Hereros. In 1897 with the Swartboois and the Afrikaners. In 1900 the Bastards, a pastoral tribe of about 5,000 descended from white hunters and Hottentot women, were goaded into rebellion. In 1903 there was rebellion among the Bondelszwartz tribe, and in the following year the Hereros commenced a bitter war which they continued for three years against the increasing military forces which the Germans poured into the country, until, of the 100,000 they had been, 80,000 men, women, and children had died or fled into kindlier lands.

The Destruction of the Hereros

During the next seven years there was no further resistance from the exhausted remnants of the natives of this pastoral land. But they had learnt what the Germans were. So, too, had all Africa's watchful millions, and it is a knowledge which may have a sombre sequel of blood if we be cowardly or criminal enough to offer Berlin a new lease of power under the pitiless Nazi creed, beside which that which went before may seem no worse than the storm of a summer day.

When war broke out in 1914, it might have been thought that the Germans in South-West Africa, isolated from their Home Country by British command of the sea, would have been content to remain quiet, in the hope that the thunder of war would only rumble in distant skies. But their ideas were different. With the psychological obtuseness which is the marvel of Germany's enemies, and the despair of her friends, they supposed that the Cape Government would seize the opportunity to break away from the Empire, or, at the least, that the Boer majority of the population would be glad to do so, and would welcome some help from them.

The Germans Invade the Cape Province

Before the close of the year, ignoring the fact that their coast settlements had fallen to the Union Defence Forces operating from the sea, they invaded the Cape Province. Joined by a rebel Dutch contingent, they fought two or three unsuccessful actions, and, within three months had been finally driven back to the South-West territory.

Having the choice between England and Germany to make, the bulk of the Cape Boers had not hesitated as to which they would prefer. Union Forces, under General Botha's skilful command, converged on the retreating Germans.

Plain Words from the Cape Government

From April to June, 1915, there was a systematic in-
exorable reduction of one settlement town after another,
until, on July 9, the German command, out-manoeuvred
and outfought, laid down its arms, and from that day the
territory has been administered by the Union Government,
which, in contrast to the hesitant attitude of the Foreign
Office in London, has said, boldly and plainly, that it has
no intention of surrendering territory which it won on the
field of battle, and where, in the first instance, it should
never have consented to the German landing.

South Africa has had an experience of German colonial methods; and she thinks one is enough.

CHAPTER XI.

Growing Prosperity

At the commencement of the war in August, 1914, there were 12,292 Germans in the South-West Territory. At its close, about half of these, including all Germans who had held official positions, were repatriated to their own country. The remainder preferred, and were unfortunately permitted, to stay.

From that date the record of the territory has been one of growing population and increasing prosperity, subject to the important qualification that the period of world depression, leading to the stagnation of the diamond export trade, caused a sharp dip which is now recovered.

The sea-borne imports for 1919 were £1,135,116; for 1936, £1,959,826. The exports for the same years rose from £1,678,554 to £3,084,168.

These figures speak for themselves. But meanwhile, a proportion of the German population which was allowed to remain has acted in a spirit of sustained disloyalty to their adopted land.

THE BRITISH COLONIES, BY S. FOWLER WRIGHT

The Attitude of the German Settlers

That there have been no serious measures of repression is due to a most tolerant patience on the part of the Union Government, such as the English population would be most unlikely to experience from the Nazis, if the territory should be returned to them.

Martial law, under which the country was at first necessarily administered, was abolished at the end of 1920, by which time all troops had, in fact, already been withdrawn, and civil courts established.

A Constitution was granted in May, 1925, which is substantially unaltered to the present day.

A Legislative Assembly of eighteen members was constituted, of which the Governor nominated six and twelve were elected. The German element of the population secured several seats in this Assembly, and actually used them, both in 1930 and 1931, to vote against this electoral body having extended powers. Their policy has been directed mainly to prevent the territory becoming a fifth Province of the Union, which the majority of its inhabitants desire.

In 1924, when the question was last raised, the German members withdrew from the Assembly and subsequently resigned. The Union was then again petitioned to accept the territory formally within its fold, subject to the conditions of the Mandate from the League of Nations under which it had consented to act.

A new election was held later in the year, after the wearing of political uniforms and the open preaching of Nazi disloyalty had been banned, and the "German Workers' Party" declared an illegal organisation; and the motion asking for admission to the Union was passed by the two-thirds majority that the constitution required.

This request the Union refused. Full membership of its federation is, it decided after two years' consideration, a privilege which the conduct of the territory as a whole has not yet earned. But administration under the mandate it will not shirk.

Seditious Activities

Unrest among German population, attempts to establish a "Hitler Youth" movement, and illegal recruiting activities, have continued, and have still been met with more patience than they deserve. An explosion of persistently disloyal elements would have been a wiser and salutary procedure.

And meanwhile, what grievances have these German settlers, or Germany, had? The answer is, less than none.

Pages could be written about the liberality of spirit in which a most liberal mandate has been administered, and the patience forbearance with which it has been sought to induce these German settlers to become loyal citizens of the South Africa they have made their home. It has been fruitless, because it is not freedom, but the domination of Berlin, which they make their aim.

Free Trade with Germany

But it should be sufficient to give one illustration of a spirit of administration which Germany certainly will not emulate if she shall ever find herself in a position to close that territory to foreign trade.

Of goods landed at South-West African ports, fifty percent come from Germany, twenty-five percent from Great Britain, and twenty percent from the United States. (There is also overland trade, of which no analysis exists.)

The fact is that we find here, as with Tanganyika, that Germany and Germans have, or can have, equality of every kind. They are free to dwell in liberty. They are free to trade. They are only not free to rebel, or to oppress the British, South African, or native races among who they live.

What more could they have, what changes could be made, which would not weigh down the scale unfairly against British, Boers, or native Africans who share the land with them, and certainly with no less than an equal right?

Even the principle of self-determination, however it be defined, will not help them, for the recalcitrant German settlers are far less numerous than the English and Boers.

The nature and effects of the mandate under which the South-West Territory is held from the League of Nations has had no more than a casual reference, because these mandates will be the subject of separate consideration. The German population have expressed their wish for the mandate to be continued, though it is difficult to see how it can be of profit to them.

Freedom in South Africa

But there is nothing on earth to prevent the whole of South Africa becoming part of the German Empire tomorrow, if it should desire to do so. It is certain that England would not fire a single shot to hold it against the will of its citizens. And that is why it is so entirely certain that such a position will not arise; and why the cause of liberty, or justice, or self-determination, or anything else worth serving would not be served by the surrender of any part of Africa, or of the British Empire elsewhere, to the tyrannous German power.

CHAPTER XII.

The West African Colonies

To complete the survey of the ex-German African colonies, it is necessary to glance briefly at two territories upon the western side of Equatorial Africa.

They were both sandwiched between French and British settlements there, were both conquered by joint French and British forces during the course of the War in Europe, and were both divided between France and England at its conclusion, with France receiving much the larger shares.

Togoland was surrendered to a Franco-British invading force immediately upon the outbreak of hostilities in August, 1914, and occupied from that date. Eight years later—in July, 1922—a League of Nations mandate confirmed an existing fact by allotting two-thirds of it, almost 22,000 sq. miles, to France, and about 11,000 square miles to Britain.

It is a fertile tropical country, with a considerable Negro population, partly suitable for plantations, but with a climate in which white men exist with difficulty, and where they cannot undertake manual labour.

Its native population has so much diversity that forty-six distinct languages are recognised as being spoken in the French territory.

British Togoland

The population of British Togoland (now under Gold Coast administration) is somewhat less varied. In 1935 it was estimated at 338,650, among whom only forty-three were non-Africans. Its exports are chiefly coco, palm-oil, rubber, copra, kernels, cocoa, and coffee, of which some are plantation grown, and others are brought in by the natives to barter for European goods. Under an unselfish British administration, state expenditure has so far exceeded income, but prosperity increases, and, with existing circumstances, it may be anticipated that its budgets will soon balance. There are now over a hundred native schools established by various missions throughout the territory, with Government support.

The Cameroons

The Cameroons were occupied by French and British troops in 1916. They were finally divided by allocating about 166,000 sq. miles to French, and 34,081 to British control; but it should be explained that the French portion included about 100,000 sq. miles which, until 1911, had been part of French Equatorial Africa, and had been ceded by France to Germany in that year, in the endeavour to satisfy Germany's clamorous demands for a "place in the sun," with which both the Quai d'Orsay and Downing

Street were so largely occupied during the thirty years preceding the war. This territory was returned to French Equatorial Africa, and the division of the Cameroon Territory remaining was therefore in the agreed proportions of two to one.

The British Cameroon Territory is now attached to Nigeria for administrative purposes. It has a comparatively dense native population of from 800,000 to 1,000,000. There is fertile plantation land near the coast and the interior is heavily forested.

Its exports are similar to those of British Togoland, with the variation that bananas are a main crop.

Like Togoland, it is unsuited for European settlement, and here also Government expenditure has, so far, exceeded revenue, while its prosperity has increased and its population multiplied.

CHAPTER XIII.

THE PORTUGUESE COLONIES

In view of the suggestions which have been made in various quarters that the ambitions of Germany might be satisfied by the surrender to them of one or both of the two principal Portuguese colonies in Africa, it may be well at this point to take a brief glance at what they are, and to consider with what aspect of decency, if any, such a transfer could be proposed.

Portugal is a country with a great past, and a future which, if European anarchy be averted, may be brighter than its more recent history.

So far as exploration, conquest, or colonisation can give good moral claim to lands which had been occupied rather than owned by great herds of beasts and less numerous of nomadic men, who were themselves hunted, if not for their actual flesh, yet to be sold into conditions of beastlike servitude, Portugal must be ranked first among European nations, where Germany has scarcely a place at all.

Not only down the western coast, but round the Cape, and as far north as Mombasa Bay, their primitive, high-

sided, thirty-five-ton vessels sailed perilously through uncharted seas. They were not idealists, but the Moslem
power which they destroyed at Diu—one of the most decisive and momentous naval battles of the Christian era—
was more ruthless than they.

As the centuries passed, their power decayed, primarily because the lower-built Dutch vessels answered the
helm better than theirs, and their influence and possessions
shrank. But they still held to wide territories in subtropical Africa—Mozambique on the eastern, and Angola
on the western coast.

During the last century they have been fortunate in the
fact that, apart from the short period during which Germany appeared on the scene, they have had in England a
surrounding neighbour who did not abuse her strength.

How they would have fared had Germany been in a
similar position may be judged from the circumstances of
a treaty negotiation of 1898.

The Portuguese colonies were then comparatively undeveloped—as they still are, and as, but for European jeal-
ousies, they need not have been expended profitably upon
them, and the stronger lure of Brazil has drawn colonisation away.

Portugal Asks for a Loan

But in 1898 Portugal was anxious to develop the resources of these African possessions, and sought a loan.
Relations between Paris and London were strained, owing
to the Fashoda incident which did not even remotely affect
the interests of Germany, but that country seized the occa-

sion to blackmail the English Government, as its habit was. It claimed a right to participate in the proposed loan to Portugal, and explained its plans.

The negotiations that followed, in which Lord Salisbury, Sir Edward Grey, Joseph Chamberlain, and Arthur Balfour each had his share of responsibility, appear monstrous when they are coolly reviewed, but this cannot be fairly done without full consideration of the difficulties of those times, which were as real and in some aspects as serious as, though they may have been different from, ours. But they are a lesson in the danger of relying on the courage and discretion of professional politicians to protect either the interests or the honour of this country, when public opinion is indifferent or ill-informed.

Germany Proposes a Plan

The German Government proposed that they should be allowed to share in the loan, but that no other European Government should be permitted to do so. The failure of Portugal to make punctual repayments was to be anticipated, and was to be made occasion for seizing the colonies, which was to be the subject of a secret agreement, made in advance, by which the two creditors would settle how they were ultimately to share the spoils.

But perhaps sharing the spoils is a barely accurate description of that which was not merely proposed but actually became a signed bargain during Lord Salisbury's illness. England did little more than retain a reversionary right to Lorenço Marques and Delagoa Bay, which, by a straightforward treaty with Portugal, she already had.

A Bargain Made

The essential element of the bargain was that Germany should seize Portugal's colonies at a future date, and that England should not interfere for their protection: the un-written consideration was that if France should make war at that time for the advancement of her interests in the Su-dan, Germany would not take the opportunity of attacking us in a quarrel with which she had nothing to do.

Germany had, at that time, no alliance nor any friend-ship with France, neither had she any difference with Eng-land. Neither her honour nor her interests were at stake. The proposal was blackmail in its crudest form. It was no honour to British statesmen that it did not succeed. A whisper of what was happening reached Portugal, the of-fered loan was prudently declined, and the Portuguese colonies remained undeveloped.

Portugal Takes Alarm

It will be observed that German methods of negotia-tion were the same under the Empire that they are now; and it is unsurprising that the German Government, whose recognition of the sanctity of treaties, or other scraps of paper (except, of course, anything which Herr Hitler and Mr. Neville Chamberlain may combine to sign in the sight of an admiring world), has always depended upon whether they were advantageous to herself, had the impudence, at more recent dates, to invoke the terms of that abortive document as binding this country to admit her prior claims upon the territory of our ally.

So, through the bad faith of this cowardly intrigue, Portugal was denied a loan which was imperatively needed in her own interests, and in that of her colonies, which she would have trusted England to make, and which would have been profitable to us. And the years passed.

The administration of these colonies, while liberal by German standards, had been deficient in many respects by ours, partly from lack of means, and partly from lower conceptions of obligation to the aborigines of exploited lands; but following the Portuguese revolution there have been evidences of a more liberal as well as a more energetic spirit.

Mozambique

Portuguese East Africa—Mozambique—has, at present, stringent laws limiting foreign European settlement. These laws certainly restrict either British or German immigration, but while the present German conception of nationality and of conduct proper to those who settle in foreign lands remains as it now is, it would be hard to say that they are more drastic than the security of the colony requires.

The white population is about 25,000, and there are nearly as many non-European immigrants, including many British Indians.

The agricultural possibilities of the territory are very great, and recent development, particularly in the cultivation of cotton, has been rapid.

There is a native population of about four millions, but the "large number of European soldiers," which, as we shall see later, are considered to be a commonplace of German colonisation, are not required either for external protection or internal order.

There is one ornamental squadron of cavalry. There are two batteries of machine-guns. There are ten companies of native infantry, with white officers. That is all.

Portugal, secure in her treaties with Britain, relies peacefully upon a surrounding neighbour who does not abuse her power. The Pax Britannica extends beyond its own Commonwealth; and it is a matter upon which our honour is vitally staked that that trust should not be betrayed.

Treaties of Arbitration

During the last hundred years England has contributed very largely to the world's peace, and particularly to that of the African continent, by submitting all territorial disputes to arbitration, and has persisted in this practice in spite of the fact that its continual, if not absolutely invariable result, has been adverse to her. In recent years there has been a tendency to hand over any territory which another nation may claim, on whatever slender grounds, without even this barren formality; and France, Italy, Portugal, and Belgium have all extended their colonial boundaries by this simple method.

It was by arbitration that England had lost Delagoa Bay to Portugal before the date of the abortive treaty negotiations already mentioned, Marshal McMahon, to whom the dispute had been referred, giving the usual decision in favour of the weaker Power. It would be pleasant, but difficult, to think that, if Germany should acquire the position in Africa that England now holds, she would be prepared to settle all differences in this peaceful manner.

CHAPTER XIV.

ANGOLA

Portuguese West Africa—Angola—has a relative temperate climate, and its upland interior is well watered, healthy, and suitable for European settlement. Like Mozambique, it has the misfortune to be adjacent to an ex-German colony, and to have been earmarked in Berlin for seizure at an appropriate time.

In proportion to its potentialities, Angola may be the least developed of any part of Africa. This is mainly due to maladministration in previous centuries, and to lack of capital during recent years. Until about a century ago, its main "industry" was the export of slaves to Brazil, and this trade did not entirely cease until a much later date. Compulsory native labour within the colony was not completely abolished until 1921.

Owing to such long-continued abuses, the native population is only about three and a quarter millions, although the colony has an area of 785,000 sq. miles, most of which is fertile. Properly developed, it could sustain ten times its present population, and still be a sparsely occupied land.

The white population is only about 7,500, of which a third are Germans, and British and South Africans combined are about equal in number. Four-fifths of the white population is in Lobito, one of the finer ports of the West African coast.

The exports of Angola, consisting mainly of coffee, maize, sugar, cotton, and other such subtropical products, tend to increase in value, and its finances are mildly prosperous. Very rich copper deposits have been located, but not yet worked.

Custom duties are heavy, especially upon goods shipped in foreign bottoms, the Portuguese policy being to encourage its own mercantile navy by this system of indirect subsidy. But the British mandated policy of holding the door wide open to German competition in the neighbouring South-West Territory has enabled a fleet of German liners to be maintained on the coast, and a maritime treaty (July, 1936) between Portugal and Germany has modified the position in favour of the latter country, although Britain had, and still holds, the larger share of Angola's foreign trade.

The colony is now far better administered than was the case ten years ago, and requires nothing but present capital and a sense of future security to advance it to the position of one of the most prosperous, as it is already one of the healthiest, parts of South Africa.

The Project of Jewish Immigration

It is particularly opportune at the present time, when the Jews in Germany and in other barbarous countries are being so severely persecuted, to observe that a project for large-scale Jewish immigration took shape in 1913, and was revived in 1934, though without immediate result.

It is doubtful whether there is a similar area, equally suitable for such a purpose and equally unpopulated, on any part of the earth's surface, and it would be far more equitable to consider such an allocation than to surrender this fertile territory to their German persecutors.

CHAPTER XV.

THE ATTITUDE OF PORTUGAL

Such are the Portuguese colonies. They are already prosperous, and of enormous potentialities. Having been under the flag of a relatively small country, they have naturally attracted German cupidity from the day when the newly-formed Empire looked 'round for anything lying loose on the world's surface on which it might lay its hands. Their protection was the Anglo-Portuguese treaties, apart from which they would scarcely have remained peaceably in the possession of their present owners.

Should Germany be able to acquire them now, by a direct and freely negotiated bargain, it is improbable that any other nation would interfere, however ominous for the future peace of Africa such a transaction might be held to be. It is therefore of importance to understand the probable attitude of the Portuguese Government to such a proposal.

That there may be no dangerous ambiguity on this point, President Carmona recently issued this statement:

Sometimes, for purposes which to us are more than suspect, the Portuguese colonies are referred to as subjects of barter. We consider them to be outside any and every agreement of any kind.

They are part of us, and together with the Mother Country constitute a single indivisible whole, which no will, whether of ourselves or of others, can mutilate.

The Portuguese Ambassador in London, Dr. Monteiro, at a dinner of the Royal African Society (February 1, 1939), said that this statement "reflects with the clarity of a mirror" the universal feeling of Portugal.

That being so, Germany could obtain these colonies, if at all, only by an act of brigandage to which England must be a passive or even an actively consenting party. It would be an action far baser even than the surrender of our own territories to the threat of violence, such as no British Government would be likely to contemplate, and which would be repudiated with indignation by the general conscience.

The possibility of it becoming a question of practical politics has appeared to be discounted by repeated more or less official declarations from Berlin that nothing different was sought from the return of the actual colonies lost. Nothing more was desired. Nothing different would be considered.

Instructions to the German Colonial League

But with the commencement of 1939 there have been indications that Germany has gained sufficient self-confidence to open a wider mouth.

The German Colonial League, of which General Ritter von Epp is president, has been agitating on this subject for more than two years past, not only in Germany but in the ex-German colonies, and very actively in this country. It has adopted the tone of assuming that the lost colonies are *de facto*, and will soon be *de jure*, parts of the Third Reich. It is actually organising a "Colonial Exhibition" to be held in Dresden during June, 1939, by which time it appears to hope, and may believe, that the colonial empire of Germany will have gained more substance than it now has.

A Bold Demand

It is exceedingly unlikely that such a body would speak or act without the approval, or indeed without the explicit instructions, of the German Government. It is therefore of extreme significance that the officials of this League have received instructions to cease agitating for the specific return of the former colonies and to substitute a demand that *all colonial possessions shall be redistributed in proportions scaled to the populations of the home countries.*

They have been instructed to argue that this radical redistribution would be no more than an act of basic justice, on the assumption that all colonies are exploited for the material enrichment of the holding country, and that Germany is morally entitled to a share in strict proportion to her population in Europe.

The proposal to effect such an adjustment is so wildly impracticable, and any initial plausibility which it may have is dependent upon so many fallacies of logic and the ignoring of so many facts, that it would be absurd to treat it seriously in itself. Yet it may be a fact of the utmost gravity that such a contention should be set up.

CHAPTER XVI.

GERMAN NEW GUINEA

A proposal to return any part of New Guinea to Germany would raise different considerations from those which prohibit disturbance of the African territories.

They are considerations vital to the existence of the British Empire, and all which that existence means to the world; and they have a special threat to Australia which may make the minority in that island continent, who recently raised the question of whether Australia would inevitably be involved in a British war, and gave it a negative reply, wishing they had said less.

Australia is the largest island in the world; the next largest is New Guinea, which lies to the north, separated by no more than the eighty miles of the Torres Strait.

Those straits are studded with small islands, between which are narrow channels through which passes the rich commerce of Australia and the Western world. The military occupation of those islands would control the straits. They are now in the possession of the Queensland Government. They are not yet seriously fortified, though this position is not likely to continue.

The Dutch Were First

The Dutch were the first to secure a foothold on the mainland of New Guinea. They occupied its western end, which was all their concern. They did not want New Guinea itself, so much as to block the way to discovery of Spice Islands further east, which might compete with theirs. English enterprise swerved southward, seeking land in a more temperate zone. In the end we came to New Guinea from the opposite direction, and landed on its eastern coast. We had not passed the Dutch barrier. We had come in at the back door. Dutch and British alike found New Guinea an uninviting land. Most of it was—and still is—covered by dense forests clothing the sides of steep gorges, narrow and deep, often soaked with torrential rains, and oppressed by a steaming heat.

The Interior

The moist, dense, luxuriant forests contain few beasts, and these are of small size, but they have a wonder of tropic flowers, and great butterflies, and bright-plumaged birds. It is a land in which the flora of Malaya and that of Australia meet in a profusion which neither parent can equal. It is inhabited by numerous scattered tribes of very diverse races, but all primitive in habits and low in intellect. There are cannibals and head-hunters there today, as there were when Thomas Forrest landed from his ten-ton galley a century and a half ago. The forests are very difficult to penetrate from their luxuriance, their moist heat, the rivers that must be crossed, and their abrupt gorges which must be continually descended and climbed while cutting blindly through tropic growth. Much of the interior is still unexplored.

New Guinea is nearly 1,500 miles in length, and averages about 500 miles in breadth. When the Germans began to look round for lands where they could stake a claim, there was Dutch settlement at the one end and British protection vaguely extending over the other, with a wide space between, the ownership of which had not been defined.

Queensland's Anxiety

Queensland had petitioned the Home Government more than once to proclaim a definite protectorate of this ill-defined territory, dreading the ultimate result if any part of it should be possessed by a foreign power other than Holland, which she felt no reason to fear. At that time it might have been done with an unchallenged right, the only necessity being to come to a friendly understanding as to where Holland's boundary met our own.

But our British Government would not move. During the latter part of the nineteenth century the principal anxiety of the Foreign Office appears to have been that they should not be considered greedy by other Powers. Foreign ambassadors in London who wished to make colonial claims found a market in which it was easy to deal.

British Foreign Office Policy

The Victorian epoch is commonly represented as one in which England acted with an arrogant sense of power. An examination of Foreign Office correspondence, and of the treaties that were made, does not support this view. There was a firm stand made occasionally, as at Fashoda, but generally any nation could have anything for which it could make out even a flimsy claim, and, where Germany was concerned, she might get it merely by mentioning her desire in a surly way, and hinting that it would be sufficient to make her a better neighbour in Europe—until she should open her mouth again.

When Tennyson wrote:

> Pray God our greatness do not fail
> Through craven fear of being great

he saw the timidity—or perhaps "misinterpreted generosity" would be more exact—with which foreign negotiations were conducted, with accurate eyes.

In 1883 the nervousness of the Queensland Government caused it to proclaim a protectorate of the south-eastern shore of New Guinea off its own bat. But the British Government actually repudiated this claim to a vacant coast, possession of which was a vital necessity for Australian security; though it was persuaded in the following year, with more reluctance than it usually showed when giving something away, to proclaim a protectorate "from the 141st meridian eastward as far as East Cape, with the adjacent islands far as Kosman Island."

The German Landing

Perhaps we should say that they *had* given something away, in the usual direction, before allowing themselves to make this declaration, for, almost immediately afterwards, Germany, although not having a foothold on the island or a valid claim of the remotest kind, announced on November 16, 1884 that the northeast part of the island was her own property, sent a landing-party to hoist the German flag, and established a trading station. It will be noticed that this is the same year in which the claims to Tanganyika and South-West Africa were made, with the support of the British Foreign Office. The year 1884 stands out as that in which these artificial "colonies" were created, and from which the present trouble began, the British Government showing as much anxiety to establish Germany as a neighbour to the overseas parts of the Empire as though she were seeking a heritage for her own babe.

When the Germans landed in 1884, there was not a single white man of any nationality in the part of New Guinea which they had claimed. It was not a case of the flag following trade or settlement, but it was to be one of very little trade following the flag.

It was simply a case of Germany wanting to say that large portions of the earth's surface belonged to her, which the British Foreign Office, instead of sitting on it with a decision which would have done much for the world's peace, preferred to nurse like a sick child. It was a case of purchasing future trouble with present ease which we may do well to ponder today.

Two Hundred Islands

Germany did not only annex the mainland; she claimed, in the same arbitrary manner, without pretexts of settlement or discovery, over two hundred islands, including the Solomon and Admiralty Groups, which became generally known as the Bismarck Archipelago.

The area of Kaiser Wilhelm's Land, as the Germans called their new mainland possession, was about 70,000 sq. miles. Twenty-two years later—in 1906—its white population of every nationality, including Germans, was *one hundred and forty nine.*

At the conclusion of the war this territory (together with the ex-German islands south of the equator, except German Samoa, which is administered by New Zealand) passed into Australia's control. Its non-indigenous population in 1937 had risen to 5,897, including: British— 3,329; U.S.A.—151; German—469; Chinese—1,525; Dutch—155; Japanese—40

There was a *known* native population of about half a million, but much of the interior is still unexplored, and may contain tribes which the forests hide.

The country is known to be rich in undeveloped mineral wealth, but mechanical difficulties of transport, particularly of heavy machinery, retard its exploitation.

The Discovery of Gold

Gold-mining beyond the frontiers of civilisation has been commenced during the Australian occupation, the precious metal having been located far in the inhospitable interior, and machinery which could hardly have been dragged through forest and gorge and swamp has been carried sectionally through the air, a fleet of planes now being in regular service between Australia and the mines.

The capital invested in this goldfield amounts to many millions. It is entirely British Empire and American money. The gold obtained has already reached an annual total of £2,000,000, and there is a probability that mining operations may extend until the prosperity of the Australian goldfields has been exceeded.

Western Samoa

Western Samoa, which is the name given to the ex-German Samoan Islands, is now governed by New Zealand, with the liberality and in the disinterested spirit which her mandate requires. The German occupation only dated from November, 1899, as the result (need it be said?) of an Anglo-German treaty by which Great Britain renounced her own claims in favour of a greedier Power.

No German who knows the facts will be ungrateful if the period of their occupation be passed over without remark.

The whole of the South Pacific Islands held by Australia and New Zealand are utterly unfortified, that being one of the conditions of the League of Nations mandates, which has been strictly observed. (Were we not all to be secure beneath the League of Nations' extended wing?)

Japan took the German Islands north of the equator under the same conditions, and has fortified some of them, without protest from our peace-loving government, in no half-hearted manner.

CHAPTER XVII.

LOOKING AHEAD

It will be well to ask ourselves, before our politicians go further upon the perilous road of discussion with Germany, what the effect of surrendering Kaiser Wilhelm's Land and the South Pacific Islands would be upon our prestige and interests in the Far East, and upon those millions of British blood who are divided from us by two oceans, but for whom Britain is still the shield of their lasting peace.

We can put aside the idea that it would be regarded as an act of altruistic justice for nations of lower moralities to admire and to imitate as occasion comes.

Even if that were true—which it would not be—it would not be believed.

It would be accepted as a decisive sign that our empire will fall apart, and that the process has begun; which is what Japan, among others, would like to think—and perhaps does.

A Japanese Opinion

Mr. Shiratori, the new Japanese Ambassador to Italy, gave an interview to a representative of the Danzig organ of Nazism, the *Neueste Nachrichten* (October 27, 1938), in the course of which he said:

> Great Britain's predominance in the Far East has come to an end for ever. A new chapter of Japanese history begins.

It is a fact so evident that even Japanese discretion does not think it injudicious to boast of it in blunt words to those who are unfriendly to us!

Well, Japan may be wrong. While the lion lives, it is premature to divide his skin. But, if it be error, it is one which such surrender to Germany would so emphatically support, that Japan would be very unlikely to unlearn it, if at all, without much shedding of British blood.

And suppose that we should lose a war in the Far East under the weakened conditions in which it would be fought? Suppose that German or Japanese armies—or both—should land from New Guinea or elsewhere in New Zealand or Australia, and should prove too numerous or too strongly equipped to be driven out?

Even then the advocates of this peculiarly new deal may argue that it would not be very serious, because, under the revised rules of warfare as they are understood by the totalitarian states, all occupied territories would be evacuated in twenty years' time. Well, perhaps. We may give New Guinea, or any other of our Far Eastern dependencies, to Germany, and tell Asia that it has been done from pure kindness of heart, but she will not believe; for the Asiatic may be an idealist—very many are—but he is not a fool.

Suggestions for Future Peace

The Japanese are a polite race, or, at least, at one time they were. New habits, new manners. There have been signs of change during recent years. But they may tell us that they can appreciate good humour as much as Germany. It will promote further amity in the Far East if we surrender Hong Kong without regrettable loss of life, which may be guaranteed providing only that we leave its "installations" intact, according to Czechoslovakian precedent, and as good feeling will naturally lead us to do.

And a quick deal after that might even save a large part of Australia for a time, if we should have the sense to withdraw from its northern half (for doing which a far stronger moral plea could be urged than for the return to Germany of colonies which are better administered in their present hands than they would be likely to be by her). And after that the issue could be left to time in the patient Oriental manner. It could be fought out between the fecund Japanese and the comparatively barren Australian women to its certain end. (Unless, of course, the women of Japan should be converted to the queer gospel which Mr. H. G. Wells urged upon them, so earnestly and vainly, twelve years ago, or those of Australia should revert to a better faith.)

Singapore might remain ours for a time, as being hard to take, and having become no more than the gate of a plundered store. But it would have become an expensive luxury to maintain, and the Japanese might agree to buy it from us at a good price, as they would be well able to do.

The liquidation of the British Empire would have begun, and a twilight of freedom would be falling upon the world.

CHAPTER XVIII.

THE FEELING IN AUSTRALIA

It is not wonderful that Australia feels as strongly antagonistic to the return of any part of New Guinea to Germany as does the Cape Union Government concerning Tanganyika or the South-West Territory. She sees a threat to her own security which she would have no power to prevent. It is easy for her to say she will not agree, while she is buying airplanes in dozens, and disputing as to whether her slowly increasing population can raise a militia of 70,000 men for the defence of her own shores. But if England should tell Germany it is hers to take, what could Australia do?

Some of its people, descendants of British-born settlers, have spoken publicly, even during the past year, as though Australia were independent of the rest of our Commonwealth, and might decide to stand back if England should be involved in a major war. But now, having come to realise how entirely dependent they are upon the strength of the British shield, and having been roused to wakefulness at a late hour, they are discussing how far New Guinea could be defended from the air, using Port

Darwin as a base. As to which the answer must be that it must depend upon how seriously it should be attacked. Without England's aid, its defence could be no more than a gallant but vain attempt.

Do they envisage a Commonwealth in which England will always be ready to protect her weaker children, but they will be free to desert her at an hour of need? Or a day when they will be stronger than she, and can stand securely apart? It may well be that such a day will come, but, if so, it is far ahead.

The Unity of the British Commonwealth

Today, except for vote-catching politicians, the question does not exist. Let the United States stand aside if she will (which some of us do not believe) when the battle of freedom joins. But the British Empire, by instinct, by loyalty, by common ideals and common speech, no less than by self-interest, is indivisibly one; and it is a fact for her foes to fear.

CHAPTER XIX.

WHAT MANDATES ARE

Having surveyed the mandated territories, it may be convenient to turn at once to consider what mandates are, and how far, if at all, they affect our own rights of possession, and Germany's claims.

The matter is of the more interest—it is scarcely of any importance, as will appear—because the Germans in South-West Africa, obviously acting on instructions from Berlin, have resisted the policy of denouncing the mandate for that territory, and have appealed to the Versailles Treaty, as Germany, though vigorously repudiating it at other times, is always ready to do in support of her own aims.

It is a treaty the obligations of which she no longer recognises, but they are to remain binding on us.

The first obstacle to clear thinking on this matter to most English people is one of definition. Very few have an even vaguely accurate idea of what a mandate is, because, though it specifies a form of contract recognised not only by the ancient Roman law but by most modern European legal systems derived therefrom, it has no place in our English code.

There is insufficient reason to turn aside here in pursuit of legal subtleties of no final importance to the issue with which we deal. We go far enough if we observe that the basic principle of this form of contract is that the party undertaking the mandate is responsible to the mandator on the sole consideration that he (the mandator) will indemnify the mandatory against loss or risk in the execution of the responsibility he has undertaken, the only exception being that the mandator has no such responsibility when the conditions of the mandate are entirely for the benefit of the mandatary. Let us therefore see exactly what these mandates are, and how far this consideration is due.

They were issued to the three mandatory Powers, England, France, and Japan, by the League of Nations, it and gave them, in radical fact, nothing at all, for they dealt with territories which had been previously conquered by, and had actually been in possession of, these Powers for some years at the time when the mandates were drawn up.

Various Forms of Mandates

There are three kinds.

Mandates A referred to Palestine and Syria, and contemplated the eventual independence of these countries. We have no present concern with these beyond remarking that, if the German colonies are "wrongfully" withheld from Germany, these are withheld from Turkey with no better right.

Mandates B applied to: Tanganyika, Togoland, and The Cameroons. They required that these territories should be administered under conditions which would "guarantee freedom of conscience and religion, subject only to the maintenance of public order and morals, the prohibition of abuses such as the slave trade, the arms traffic, and the liquor traffic, the prevention of the establishment of military or naval bases or fortifications, and of military training of the natives for other than police purposes and the defence of their own territories, and secure equal opportunities for the trade and commerce of other members of the League."

Mandates C applied to: German New Guinea; The Pacific Islands now held by Australia, New Zealand, and Japan; Nauru, a small phosphate-producing island held by Great Britain; and South-West Africa. These were defined as territories which, owing to sparseness of population, small size, remoteness from centres of civilisation, or geographical contiguity, can best be administered under the laws of the mandatary as integral portions of its territory, subject to the safeguards already enumerated in the interests of the indigenous populations."

It will be seen that none of these conditions was of any possible benefit to the mandatory Powers. They voluntarily accepted restrictive obligations upon territories captured from Germany in a war in which they had incurred enormous losses, which were already in their possession, in the altruistic spirit in which the League of Nations was formed; and these conditions Great Britain and the Dominions concerned have scrupulously observed—have, indeed, more than observed, against their direct interests, for the obligations to allow freedom of trade only applied to

League members, and they have been permitted to Germany and Japan, to the grave detriment of Empire commerce, after they have left the league.

The Responsibility of the League

But as it is apparent that the conditions of the mandates were entirely in the interests of the inhabitants of the territories, and of League members other than the mandataries, it follows that the mandator—that is, the League of Nations—is legally committed to protect the holders of these mandates from all risks arising therefrom, or, in the absence of such protection, that the mandates are legally void. For how (for instance), can a mandatary be seriously required to hold its territory unfortified by stipulation of the mandator, unless that mandator be prepared and adequate to undertake its defence? Yet Great Britain, in spite of the League's consistent refusal to honour such obligations, and its substantial collapse, has scrupulously observed this condition, and, even now, Australia is planning the defence of New Guinea only from points outside the mandated territory.

But would the League of Nations indemnify us from any German attack? Would its component nations fight on our behalf? Would they finance any operation which the upholding of these mandates might involve? Are they doing that with Palestine now?

The frailty of this obligation to the League of Nations could be pursued to final absurdity down many paths, but they would be waste of words.

Neither by any law, nor any principle of moral equity, does obligation exist. For the League of Nations gave nothing to us. We voluntarily agreed to limit, and do limit, our conquest rights, against guarantees which have become valueless, the contracting parties (who, in the event, would not have fulfilled them) having faded away.

It is necessary to make this clear, because there is a widespread feeling that we are merely custodians of these mandated territories; that they have never been more than loosely attached to the British Empire; and that we may lightly resign that which has never been held in our own right.

It would be a two-edged argument, for that which is not ours to hold could not be ours to give. But, be that as it may, it has no substance. It is enough to observe that it would be of no benefit to Germany if it had.

A German Error?

The idea that Germany appears to encourage, and which, if it were true, would explain her instructions to the Germans in South-West Africa to resist any alteration in the status of that territory by which its mandate would be ignored, is that by some process, direct or indirect, she had herself made over her colonies to the League. But that is not the fact, and even if she could logically invoke treaties in her own interest which she repudiates on other issues, it would not help her at all.

By the Treaty of Versailles (Art. 119) Germany resigned all claims on these colonies unconditionally in favour of "the principal allied and associated Powers," and from that moment their final destiny was a matter for the allies to settle among themselves, as they proceeded to do. The legal questions which might be raised as between these Powers and the League, if the League were a body *continuing to function and equal to discharging its obligations, which it is not*, would be extremely complex, if not insoluble by anything but a surgical process. But they would certainly be of no assistance to Germany, nor, as she is not a member of the League by her own will, do they concern her in any way.

Mr. Eden's View

Even Mr. Eden, who so long and ably fought the impossible Geneva battle, and who should be able to explain these matters if any can—the League of Nations being his attractive, anaemic pet—confessed both himself and the British Government to be baffled by the complexities of the juridical problem when he said in the House of Commons (July 27, 1936):

> The question of any transfer of mandated territories would inevitably raise grave difficulties, moral, political, and legal, to which His Majesty's Government must frankly say that they have been unable to find any solution.

Finally, the United States

As a final comic-opera complexity, there are treaties with the United States so worded that England could legitimately contend that she would have no right to vary the terms of the mandates (and therefore no right to transfer the mandated territories to Germany or any other country) without the consent of that Government.

So, if we pursue the legal absurdity of the position to its final lair, we can envisage the possibility of England and the League of Nations professing their willingness to surrender these colonies to German importunity, and only prevented by the refusal of the United States to sanction the transfer, which, in view of their possible menace to South America, as well as on humanitarian grounds, would be a reasonable attitude for her to adopt. Whereupon the natural sequel would be for Germany and the United States to go to war to settle the issue, while the rest of the world would look on.

CHAPTER XX.

The Plea of Justice

If we can imagine a Court of International Justice, having real and recognised authority, and that Germany should bring a suit before it for the return of these territories, we can see that England, apart from the right of conquest (which surely neither Germany nor her Italian partner, busily trying to gnaw some meat from his Abyssinian bone, would soberly deny), could raise almost endless points of international law by which the plaintiff would be non-suited, or difficulties of procedure which would be hard or hopeless to overcome.

For the plain fact is that, while there might be many points to be cleared up by the "Allied and Associated Powers" among themselves, Germany is the one country which could establish no *locus standi* at all.

She did not appeal to justice when she invaded Belgium in 1914. She appealed to arms.

The verdict went against her in the court of her own choice, and she paid a far milder penalty than she would have exacted from beaten foes.

Not Justice, but Arms

She will not appeal to justice now, which would deride her claim. She will appeal to arms once more, as she has just done over Czechoslovakia. There has been no restraint of justice in the violation of the boundaries of that ancient country.

Because it consented, and we who took and then abandoned its part consented, to be defeated without a battle, its conquest was no less a military operation.

There may have been wisdom in that surrender. Or there may not. But there was no honour. And the tribunal was one at which justice did not preside. "We avoided war by threatening it," Dr. Goebbels declared, in a burst of candour, at Reichenburg (November 20, 1938).

Its danger for the world's peace—and for the existence of Nazism—is that the pitcher which goes often to the well will be broken at last. For it will surely be the destruction of Germany if her bluff be called before she has reached far more than her present strength. And if she thinks she will have Mussolini's loyal help in her hour of need—well, she may; or she may have something further to learn!

Losing Czechoslovakia, we lost some honour and a loyal friend. It is natural that we should be invited to lose more.

To claims so advanced there can be only one possible reply, which even our present Government could be trusted to make; but during recent years Germany, who, when she does not bluster is always disposed to whine, has advanced a plea on grounds other than those either of peace or of international law; and though it is one which could have been more powerfully urged had she remained a member of the League of Nations, continuing as unarmed as England would also have been, and loyal to those ideals which the League has professed and partially obeyed, it is still one which should not be ignored.

A More Plausible Plea

She claims that her position as a European power without colonies places her at a disadvantage economically, and particularly so in obtaining supplies of raw materials which her industries need, and she contends that she cannot be expected to be a peaceful and friendly neighbour while this injustice persists.

This argument has impressed many who, without giving the problem any close examination, have been disposed, from generous love both of peace and of fair play, to blame the harshness of a treaty they have not read, and to say: "Why not give some of them back?" as though it were as simple as cutting a slice of cake.

It is important therefore to consider whether; this be a genuine grievance. Is Germany short of raw materials? If so, why? And how far, if at all, is that position (if it be a fact in itself) due to the alienation of German colonies twenty years ago? It would require much space, and a wide diversion from our immediate subject, to deal with these questions comprehensively, for which fortunately there is no occasion, because the most cursory examination of the problem will show that their return could make no material difference to her facilities for obtaining these supplies, and none at all except to the *direct detriment of the present prosperity of those unfortunate lands*.

Germany Has Free Access Now

The position would be slightly—but only slightly—different had tariff barriers been set up, to the disadvantage of German trade. But that has not been done. *She trades in those territories as freely as though they were hers, both to buy and sell.*

Legal possession could be of no economic benefit except so far as she should erect tariff barriers which do not now exist, or tax those lands for her own benefit, which would be the opposite of our own procedure.

Indeed, the argument is based on the assumption that a colony is to be controlled, not for its own good, but for that of the country to which it is unfortunate enough to belong.

It is not wonderful that those who dwell in these jeopardised lands do not appreciate the idea, nor that trade has languished, and all projects of development become suspended, at the mere suspicion that England may be planning to cast them off.

Raw Materials

In actual fact, Germany is not, need not be, and has not been, short of raw materials. The disciplined industry of her people has secured for themselves an export trade which gives them ample of the foreign exchange which the financing of such purchases requires, and this sufficiency has been augmented by an extreme frugality of honour in dealing with their external debts.

The shortages which they have experienced have been *the direct result of buying excessive quantities of such raw materials as are required for the manufacture of munitions of war.*

If we are foolish enough to assist them further in that direction, while they continue to obey their present truculent rulers, the man who warmed a snake in his bosom might reasonably decline our society, as that of people whose mental balance is more upset than his own.

But if Germany *has* any legitimate grievances of this kind, if tariff barriers, or difficulties of exchange, retard her or any other European country from obtaining requirements in needed quantities, or at equitable prices, then it may well be a part of Mr. Chamberlain's appeasement programme to enquire what they may be, and to organise international action for their prompt removal.

And, if so, let it be fairly done. Is Germany the only country to be appeased? It may be found that there are other quieter, smaller, countries in Europe which have juster cause of complaint.

And let the method of relief be less crude than that of giving the territories where such materials are produced to Nazi tyranny and exploitation, which would be to mock justice and freedom, and to produce a remedy far worse than the disease which it would so crudely cure.

The Argument of Bad Faith

There is one other argument sometimes advanced on the German side which hardly deserves mention, and certainly no extended refutation. It is a suggestion, usually implied rather than expressed, that Germany was led to surrender the colonies under false promises and representations that were not kept.

This is vitally false. It is also imprudent, because they were already in British and French hands when the war ceased; and it is historic fact—it is Hitler's own admission—that Germany was not a position to bargain. Her armies were in confused retreat, with their "home front" equally and irretrievably broken.

The Versailles treaty was signed—it again Hitler's own contention—under duress; from which he goes on to conclude that its provisions are not binding upon Germany. It is a difficult and dangerous theory, because its logical conclusion is that it is impossible to make any binding treaty with a defeated foe. Such a treaty binds the victor, but not vanquished!

But if the treaty were dictated, the element of bargaining did not arise; and, be that as it may, it will be useless to search the Versailles treaty for any bargains about these colonies which have not been kept, for they are not there.

Continuing Unrest

The German Government is, however, right in its contention that so long as this question of returning colonies to her remains open, there will be no rest in Europe. To which it may be added that, if their demands should be granted, there will be unrest over a much wider area.

Rest will only be possible, if at all, when Germany realises that she is asking for something she will not get.

It becomes important, therefore, to examine any real grievances that she may have, either regarding raw materials, exchange currency, or emigration, and to remove them thoroughly.

If there be no such grievance, it is almost equally important to demonstrate that fact to all impartial minds.

It is a subject on which, if the allegation be seriously urged, an international conference might reasonably be held.

CHAPTER XXI.

THE RESPONSIBILITY FOR TODAY

The Treaty of Versailles, and the League of Nations which was its child by President Wilson, were intended to inaugurate an era of peace and international justice on earth, which they did do.

But, beyond any of the contracting ties on either side, England can plead at the bar of history that the responsibility was not hers, and she is guiltless, to the same extent, of responsibility for the present shadow that lies over Europe, unless it be blame to her that she did interfere when Germany commenced to re-arm on a scale which would be an evident threat to the world's peace if it were allowed. There was a time when the mere threat of blockade would have been enough. But it has gone now.

She preferred—and there was more to be said for that course in advance of the event than there is now—to continue the example of disarmament, and the policy of conciliation, in a world which became less and less responsive to pacific influences.

The Failure of the League

The League of Nations had been rejected by the United States, refused by Germany, condemned by Italy and Japan, and was being used by France for meaner ends than it had been intended to serve, while England stood by it still, with an idealism only faintly reflected in the policies of smaller nations, which had thought less of saving the world than of gaining protection for themselves under diminishing shadow.

British Disarmament

England remained unarmed in an arming world to her own peril, and her reward was nothing better than the insult of Italy, the destruction of Abyssinia, and the surrender of Munich; but it was an error of magnanimity, and she may use the sword at last in a firmer hand because she had shown that she was ready to lay it down.

The ghost of the League still walks, but from the moment when its members declined to go to the aid of Manchuria—when she was first worried by Japan—was utterly and finally wrecked.

It has bleated since as the wolves have pulled three of its members—Abyssinia, China, and Czechoslovakia—out of the fold, wondering which will be next on the butchers' list. But when did bleating save the life of a single sheep?

America Killed the League

The League was, in fact, impotent from that historic moment—supremely important in the history of our civilisation—when the Senate of the United States repudiated the pledge which President Wilson had given on his country's behalf.

In the imperfect Treaty of Versailles—so much and so ignorantly abused—there was the germ of a great hope for the world.

But the growth of that seed depended upon its cultivation by the United States and the British Empire—the only true friends among the Great Powers that it ever had—and which the United States proved itself too provincial to take that place in the world's Councils which is its right—when it became clear that it was "not great enough for its own destiny"—the League of Nations was no more than a broken dream.

We may hope that it will be dreamed again to the end which its founders sought. But a broken dream is difficult to resume.

The Rectitude of the American Senate

The American Senate acted within its constitutional rights, and President Wilson had exceeded his; but it was no less that the course which was chosen left the honour of a great nation indelibly stained; and it was one of those blunders which are proverbially worse than crimes.

Without President Wilson's impotent nobility Europe might have felt its hesitant way forward to something better than we now face. Or, with the whole-hearted co-operation of the great democracy of the New World, we might have come to a wide peace, in which event the Washington Government would not be looking both West and East at horizons of rising storm, and uneasily arming now.

These may sound to be hard words, but they are true; and they are written by one who knows the United States, and loves that country nearly as well as his own land.

America Collects Its Debts

Blind to a future, which the discord of its President and Senate had done so much to shape, America settled down to collect debts!

She would not listen to the advice of England—the other great creditor nation—that the cancellation of those monstrous edifices of liability would be the best healing treatment they could give the world, and from which they would not the last to benefit. Stubbornly, she thrust the world and herself forward to financial chaos, her states-men driven from below, and half-unconscious of what they did.

She refused goods. She must have gold. She had 1929.

Her government now sees with far clearer eyes. But are her people wiser today?

CHAPTER XXII.

A GERMAN PLEA

In its issue of October 20, 1938, the *Berliner Tageblatt* published an article entitled: "The White Man's Destiny," by Dr. von Ungern-Sternberg. Its theme is Germany's large and increasing population, and it argues that these numbers give a legitimate claim to the possession of overseas territory.

"Germany's population," he says, "including the regions recently acquired, amounts to nearly 80,000,000." He also stresses its (relatively) high birth-rate, and he claims that these circumstances render it "intolerable" that such a nation should be denied "possibilities of colonial expansion," and expresses the opinion that no French or English politician who is capable of clear thinking will question this.

There is a sense in which most people may agree with his argument. If a virile nation have a high birth-rate, it will require more space for its sons than that with which a previous generation may have been content, and for other nations—and particularly those of wide empty spaces and inferior fecundity—to deny them this would be asking for the trouble that they would be certain to have.

But when Dr. Ungern-Sternberg descends to detail, his conception is of a more disputable particularity.

The German Concepts of Colonies

"Without," he says, "*a large number of* settlers, pioneers, and European soldiers, no colonial power can hold her overseas possessions for a prolonged period." (Italics not his.)

It is certainly true that any country, overseas or not, requires inhabitants, and—incidentally—it is in that particular that Germany's previous efforts at colonisation were only moderately successful, of which the New Guinea figures, already given, are an emphatic proof. But that a large number of European soldiers are not needed for a colony which is equitably governed, even though it may have a large aboriginal population, is shown from figures also given previously regarding Tanganyika. It may be doubted whether, at the moment that this is written, there are more than five or six score white soldiers or police in the whole of that wide and contented territory.

A Reasonable Condition

The surplus population of Germany would—on one reasonable condition—be welcomed in many lands. There is room for them in the United States, in Australia, in South Africa, in several South American republics; and a score of other partially developed countries either do, or should, hold their doors wide open for settlers of good character, which most Germans are.

But they may ask—it is a most reasonable request—that those who come shall not enter in a spirit of aggressive nationalism, but shall be prepared to show some moderate measure of loyalty their adopted land.

Even Dr. Ungern-Sternberg might recognise, if he should reflect upon it, that those of whatever ancestral blood who now regard Africa as their home, might not welcome the idea of a "large number of...European soldiers" being introduced to that continent, and might wonder what their activities were expected to be.

Germany would doubtless reply that she is not satisfied for her surplus population to migrate to the United States or South America under their present governments. She prefers that they should go to territories which she can control from Berlin, and which she can keep exclusively to herself.

But if this were in any way possible to arrange without injustice to others, would it be desirable, either for herself or the world's peace?

It is true that such a conception of colonial possessions was once prevalent in Europe; but England, for the last half-century has been leading the way to cast it off, and it is rightly demoded now.

Even in a previous century, when British settlers in what is now the United States quarrelled with the Home Government, there was a large proportion of English people whose sympathies were with those who rebelled, and their influence did much to affect the result of, and to shorten, that fratricidal conflict.

But, what was clear to them then, Germany has not learned today. Her conception of a colony as something to be governed and exploited for her own gain, and to be a point of military advantage to vex her foes, is an evil dream from which the rest of Europe is entirely or half awake.

When it became known in England two years ago that the Nazi Government, while contemning Christianity as a religion inadequate to the new ethical standards which it would teach, was disposed to look tolerantly upon the revival of the worship of Thor, the aspect of comedy which it certainly had may have obscured its more serious meaning. The Nazi gospel will lead us back, if it can, to the twilight of civilisation, and it looked round, with a natural instinct, for an appropriate god.

CHAPTER XXIII.

EQUAL JUSTICE FOR ALL?

If it be a sound argument that because 80,000,000 Germans have a fairly high birth-rate some large overseas territories should be given to them for exclusive colonisation, then it appears to be a sound corollary that a smaller European nation, having a similar population problem, should also have an exclusive territory measured to its own scale.

A group of the various nationalities of Eastern Europe, including Poland, might aggregate a claim equal to anything which Germany could advance, and with an equal argument of having no colonies of their own.

Let us suppose that Mr. Chamberlain's anxiety for the appeasement of Europe were to be extended to them, and that there were a plan for the irrigation of the Sahara Desert—very far from an impossibility—and that it were proposed to apply it to the use of these nations for the opportunities of expansion which they require.

There would be alternative methods of allocation to be considered. The whole area might be thrown open equally to all, or it might be divided into the appropriate number of smaller restricted territories, to each of which one nation would send its surplus population to continue the ancestral culture in its exclusive domain.

The latter plan would have much immediate sentimental support, but who, looking impartially on, could call it the better way?

In the name of liberty it would have imposed numberless and needless restrictions. It would reduce the area of free choice within which a man might settle according to his own proclivities, and the occupation he might be most fitted to pursue. With every possible effort to arrive at equitable division, it would be inevitable that some of new settlements should be inferior to others in climate or fertility, some further from trading facilities of port or river.

And what would the position be likely to be in a century's time? Where there might have been growth of a strong, contented, prosperous nation, which each contributory element would have enriched, there would most probably be a group of small, jealous, divided states, with a dark record of quarrels and wars, contained within barbed-wire frontiers, and with customs barriers reducing their prosperity by restricting trade. Or perhaps their barriers would have been cleared away, and their differences forgotten, after they had passed through the bitter ordeal of a decisively conquering war.

The Example of Canada

The English of Vancouver and the French of Québec are of different races and creeds, and even in language they are apart; but they dwell in a political amity, not of common bondage, but common freedom.

It is a conception which has not yet penetrated to the German mind, and which cannot do so while Nazism remains its political creed, and there is no freedom of discussion throughout the land.

CHAPTER XXIV.

THE EXPULSION OF JEWS FROM GERMANY

The contention that because Germans have a growing population they can reasonably demand that the colonies of other nations shall be transferred to their flag can be shown to be fallacious on many grounds, but it is particularly vulnerable to one argument which their own conduct supplies.

They have been so pitilessly active in their persecutions and expulsions of their fellow-citizens of Jewish blood that they must, by that means, be effecting a reduction in population sufficient to counter-balance their natural increase for a good many years to come, so that they have themselves removed one of the main arguments on which they rely, while giving a convincing demonstration of their unfitness to govern any people of alien blood.

They have also made it a matter of elementary justice that, if any part of the earth's surface be for gift or sale, it should be put at the disposal of these pathetic exiles rather than at that of those who, by their treatment of them, have demonstrated their unfitness to exercise authority, even in their own land, and how great a crime it would be to aliens, of whatever colour, under their oppressive power.

CHAPTER XXV.

THE INEVITABLE END

The question of the growth of populations, both of the white nations relatively to each other, and to darker races, is, of course, that which will finally determine the proportions of the earth's surface which they will continue to occupy; and the constantly improving means of transit must materially hasten the process of this distribution, which the post-war tyranny of the passport system will be inadequate to resist, until there be a complete conquest of the earth's surface, at present so partially tamed to the use of man. Unless, which both by precedent and present indications may be regarded as the more probable sequel, our civilisation shall relapse to barbarism, and our descendants recommence the climbing of a ladder the top of which mankind is not destined to reach.

Apart from that possibility, those who now occupy the fairest and most temperate portions of the earth's surface cannot expect to be left in peaceful occupation unless they either throw their lands open to other races, or populate them with children of their own blood.

Nature abhors a vacuum; and not all the scientists who were ever born could make the course of existence easy for those who defy so fundamental a law.

The Example of Tunisia

Nowhere is the consequence of birth-prevention, as it must affect nationality at last, more simply and convincingly illustrated than in Tunisia, where the French rule a land in which they are outnumbered by men and women of Italian blood.

Many of the French settlers who should be there today *were not born,* and the future, now that a neighbouring territory is being systematically colonised by Italian peasants, is sombre for France.

She may see now—but even now it may be too late—that a nation's ultimate strength is not in Maginot lines, or even in thousands of bombing planes—we may become in time sufficiently civilised to abolish them—but in the abundance of its own youth.[2]

---

[2]This was written before the present Italian agitation for the transfer of the protectorate of Tunis to its own authority had begun. See Final Chapter.

According to the March, 1936, census there are some 108,000 French and 94,000 Italians inn Tunisia—about 15% of a total population of 2,600,000—the Moslems being about 85%. In 1881 there were roughly 12,000 Italians in Tunisia, while the French were only a few hundreds. In the Great War 35,000 natives gave their lives for France.

The Effects of Birth Restriction

It has been one of the facile arguments of the birth-restrictionists that women cannot be expected to produce children to become "cannon-fodder" for the next war. It is not, on any ground, a plea which will endure ethical or practical examination, and it can only come from the lips of those who are foolish or insincere; but, beyond that, it is fallacious, even in its own assumptions. It is a simple conclusion that those who are few are the more likely to perish, and that the nation which restricts the lives of its sons may thereby consign to death or ignominy those whom it is frugal to have.

It seems, indeed, a proposition too obvious for discussion or disbelief, but the white races are preferring to learn it in the school of experience, where the tuition is sound, and the fees are correspondingly high.

A Cause of German Confidence

The German journalists who prepared the minds of their fellow-countrymen for the war of 1914 stressed the point that the French nation had ceased to increase, as the Germans of that period did. They argued therefrom that the French were a decadent people, fit only to be overcome by those of more virile stock. This belief was a proximate cause of that war. It gave confidence to those who ordered the German mobilisation. And, but for the intervention of England, the anticipated overthrow of France, with whatever consequences, would certainly have occurred.

It may not be an argument of any present logical force—and could only become so in the event of men of German race being unreasonably excluded from other parts of the earth's surface, which is unlikely to occur so long as they are content to become good citizens of their adopted lands—but it holds a warning which it would be well for ourselves to heed, whether we go forward to the peace we hope or the war we have more cause to expect.

The American Illustration

Five years ago the writer stood on a high ridge of the great mountain range that looks eastward over the Californian desert. A dealer in "real estate," in the American idiom, was beside him.

Far below, the desert could be seen for hundreds of miles in the clear air of those regions, brown and level and bare, with an occasional green spot where a well had been sunk and a fruit ranch flourished.

This conversation passed:

"I suppose if sufficient boring were done, the whole desert might become fertile?"

"Yes. If you go deep enough there's no lack of water there."

"It seems a pity it isn't done."

"But while the population of California doesn't increase...?"

There was no answer to that.

CHAPTER XXVI.

SELF-DETERMINATION

There is, as an abstract question, much to be said for the principle of self-determination. It was one of the more altruistic aims—most imperfectly realised—of the Trianon Treaty, and is an argument in continual use in Germany, though it is conveniently ignored whenever its application would conflict with the real aims of the Nazi Government. The Alps (for the moment) are a barrier set by God, though the Bohemian Mountains proved to be of an inferior sanctity.

It is not an argument of any avail to them on our present issue, unless appeal be absurdly made to the ghostly votes of those who were in the German colonies twenty years ago, to the ignoring of those who are alive in them today; and even then it would be necessary that the voices of the native populations should not be heard.

But we have already observed that the multiplication of these ethnological boundaries, however well intended, may have very dubious effects upon individual liberties, and be directly disastrous to the cause of peace.

It rallies and solidifies contentious entities, and when they quarrel it may substitute bullet and bomb for the polling-booth contests by which their differences might otherwise be resolved with no less, if no more, probability of justice resulting.

To realise this, it may be enough to consider what the probable consequences would have been had Germany won the last war, and insisted upon the political separation of the various nationalities that our island contains.

Trying It on Ourselves?

Would it have been of any practical advantage to the Highland Gaels that they should have been given the separate government of their barren moors, and the separate management of their own limited finances? Would the Lowland Scots have appreciated the fact that they could hold no office of state in what had become a foreign land?

Would the tariff barriers which must have led to the policing of the Scottish borders, and the long frontier of Wales, have advanced good feeling or fostered trade? Would not the definition of the Welsh boundary, in particular, have led to questions of insoluble difficulty? To which country would the County of Monmouth justly belong?

There would have been twenty years of dispute, recrimination, and difficult adjustments, which we may think would have been settled without actual violence, but political deterioration would have been inevitable, and it is hard to think that any advance would have resulted in civil liberties or the standards of social life.

Federation Is the Better Way

The need of Europe is for federation rather than accentuation of the many differences of race, religion, and language which are its ancestral curse; and it would be an evil service to humanity to transport these racial antipathies to be fresh causes of war at future times in far-distant lands.

Surely, whatever may be said (which is much) for keeping these old cultures intact in their native lands, and their stocks pure, it is in every way better that they should blend when they go abroad, to form nations of the new vigour that such interbreeding gives, with possibilities of wider sympathies in the succeeding generations, and more general peace.

CHAPTER XXVII.

THE FRIENDSHIP OF THE GERMAN PEOPLE

It is a common argument among those whose well-founded hatred of war operates to the detriment of their logical faculty that the German people are individually friendly to ourselves, and that the thought of conflict is no more antipathetic to us than it is to them; and they conclude from this alleged fact that we have only to meet them in a spirit of conciliation for the dove of peace to appear from a cloudless sky.

Taking the alleged fact first, we may, with some qualifications, agree. Few can have travelled in Germany during recent years without meeting pleasant evidences of a desire for peace between our peoples, and, in some instances, an active desire to detach our sympathies from France to herself. It is true also that a very large proportion of the German people do not desire another war, including an enormous majority of those who are old enough to have had bitter experiences in the last.

German and Italian Antipathies

It is also, and in the end may prove to be importantly, true that the Italian and German peoples are not natural allies. The Germans are hated in Italy, and in Germany the Italians are frankly despised.

But the first of these observations must be qualified by the fact that the male youth of Germany has been reared in an atmosphere of hate, and trained to brutality, the effects of which are seen in the savage mobbing of Jewish women and men, which, even if these unhappy people were actual criminals, would be a disgrace to any civilised land.

So far as it be true that German people are averse from war, or friendly to us, it increases the tragedy of the position, but how far does it otherwise alter it in any practical manner?

We may suppose—or we might despair of humanity—that there were many Germans who disapproved of the Nazi assassinations of hundreds of patriotic Austrians—"suicides" as Nazi humour described them—but was that of any avail to those who fell to the Nazi bullets?

The Wisdom of Facing Facts

It is soundly argued that we should neither attempt to impose our own ideologies upon foreign states, nor resent the fact that theirs are of a different pattern. But when a state is guided absolutely by one man or one group, then, so long as its citizens submit to that control, we must ignore them, for they have become negligible by their own choice, and consider only the characters and intentions of those wielding so vast a power.

It was that fact which rendered the Franco-Russian Treaty so valueless in itself from the day it was signed, and so repugnant to millions of the friends of France.

We have no quarrel with Russia, and certainly none with its people, whether we consider their condition to be an occasion for envy or pity. We have no wish to interfere with their social experiments. But we must observe the actions of the men by whom they are entirely controlled, and whose guidance they would follow into any war in which those leaders might decide to engage.

A Worthless Treaty

No one who is aware of the character of the present Government of Russia, as revealed by its public actions, can sanely suppose that, if war broke out in Europe tomorrow, its attitude would be controlled by anything but its own immediate interests, or that it would be influenced in the slightest degree, one way or other, by the fact that it had entered into a treaty with Paris some years earlier.

It is that fact which made the treaty worthless, and worse than that, because alliance with the present Government of Russia, however indirect, is distasteful to millions of British people—both in Great Britain and the Dominions—not on ideological but on purely ethical grounds. The political theories which these men profess may be of the wisdom of Solomon, but they have a habit of murder which we dislike.

The Question of Confidence

And when we are asked not to make a critical position more difficult by doubting the sincerity of any declaration which Herr Hitler may make, we may appreciate the spirit of the request, and still find that the difficulty is not removed. We may be willing to give him the benefit of the doubt, but what doubt is there with which to deal?

It is no question of ideologies. It is the cold fact that Hitler's word has been proved worthless time after time before.

Even to mention this is considered injudicious by those who are already prepared to have our freedom of speech and pen curtailed to the Berlin mode.

One of the Kentucky Minstrels argues that though he may be a liar, he still may be sensitive about being so described, and it is possible that the Leader of the incomparable Nordic race may have an equally thin skin.

But the fact is beyond dispute; and it would be at our extreme peril that we should decline to recognise it. His public lying has been emphatic and circumstantial. It has been his chosen road to his political goals.

He made a public statement, which no one had asked him to do, that he would never violate the integrity of Austria; and, while he said it, he was plotting the violation of that unfortunate land.

He made the same statement about Czechoslovakia, and the same procedure followed.

It has become a formula, showing the direction to which his eyes are turned, and it has the same value as the growl of a hungry beast.

If we accept statements in *Mein Kampf* more confidently, it is not because we wish to believe evil—and they are of very sinister import for the world's peace—it is because so many of them have been confirmed by the events that followed. The credence we give to those which are still to come shows that we are willing to accept Herr Hitler's word, if he will give us any solid ground for such confidence. But it is an unfortunate fact, which no blinking of eyes can change, that if he were to swear, by whatever gods, that, if we should give him the colonies, he would continue their present decencies of administration, or that he would not arm the native populations to attack their neighbours, his word would be worth nothing. A lie may bring immediate profit, but that worthlessness is its future price.

The Practical Difficulty of Disarmament

This characteristic of the present ruler of Germany is one of the major tragedies of Europe's position today. It would remain a practical hindrance to disarmament, even though all Germany's real or alleged grievances were removed, and she were actually sincere in intending peace. It would be particularly dangerous to enter into an air-pact with her, unless there were a strictness of supervision to which she would be unlikely to submit.

The German armament manufacturers have been trained already in concealment of what they do; and three or four years ago, when the haste and energy of military preparations were already evident to anyone with average intelligence and open eyes who passed through the country, Hitler will not forget the fact—and neither should we—that the English Government (not widely different in its composition from that of today) concerned itself only to deny that Germany was re-arming at all, and to obstruct the circulation of any book which was bad mannered enough to expose that which they were resolved they would not see.

Looking at the condition of Europe today, even they may perceive that to "cry peace where there is no peace" may be a very dangerous game.

But no one who has read *Mein Kampf* can easily doubt that, if the rest of Europe should agree upon a programme of disarmament, the temptation to Hitler to use the chance for the world-domination of which he dreamed when he was an obscure man would be very great.

CHAPTER XXVIII.

OF THOSE WHO DIED

It is commonly said that if those whose lives were lost in the last war can see the sequel of what they did, they must conclude that they died in vain.

Perhaps they can; and perhaps they do so conclude. But can we be sure that their reasons would be the same as appear decisive to those by whom this remark is most often made?

Some of them supposed that they fought for freedom of thought and speech, and for the integrity of an Empire which meant that, and other things which seemed valuable to them.

May they not have thought that they died in vain as they watched Germany re-arm in the midst of a Europe which lacked courage to interfere? As they watched her plot to bring a new blight of tyranny on the world? As they saw statesmen of the great democracies do nothing to suppress the peril while it could have been done at a modest cost, and that they were only concerned to persuade themselves, and to tell the foolish people who gave them trust, that there was no cause for alarm?

It would be an excellent thing for humanity if it could end war, and no one could have a greater purpose for which to die. But it is mere cant to say that they did that. They no more fought to end war than to deflect the course of the moon.

They fought to prevent Germany bestriding a prostrate world, as she aimed to do, and they gave their lives for a purpose which did not fail.

Inter alia they fought to prevent Germany possessing herself of tropical Africa, for which she had drawn her plans, and they succeeded in that. If we surrender it now, at the mere sound of Hitler's hysteric scream on the air, they may see indeed that their sacrifices were vain for us, if not for their own souls. They might say with Rua:

> I died a death for a man. I had given the
> life of my soul to save an unsavable clan.

Much that is spoken over their graves at each Armistice Day Anniversary may, or may not, be pleasing to God; but it clearly blasphemes the dead.

CHAPTER XXIX.

NAZI INTOLERANCE

The plain fact is that Nazism is incompatible with the liberty of any non-German population over which it may gain control. For a German who regards it as admirable, it may give freedom of a kind, but it is merciless, not only to its opponents, but to those whom it regards as inferior in the racial scale—which includes all the inhabitants of the earth (except, quaintly enough, not only the Italians, but the Japanese!) who lack the advantage of German blood.

No argument of equity could give it licence to extend its intolerant rule over those who have known the blessings of freer air.

Let us, at least, avoid the cowardice of calling a base act by a better name.

If any of the ex-German colonies be returned to her it will not be an act either of justice or wisdom; for no one reasonably well informed can suppose that it will benefit either us or them, or even tend to the enduring peace of the world. Like the abandonment of Czechoslovakia by France, it will be an act of fear.

The After-Effects of Surrender

It may also commence the breaking up of a Commonwealth of Nations which will have shown itself lacking either in strength or courage to guard those who are in its pale, for the British Empire is too rich, and as yet too empty, of heritage to be held by a timid race. And if it fail, the twilight of human liberty will not be distant to fall.

For if we yield these or other lands and their peoples to the importunities or threats which we are likely to hear in the coming months, it will be because we have the fear of a German pistol against our ribs, and it will be to the sound of the world's laughter that we shall attempt to give it a nobler motive than that.

Let us quail to force if we lack manhood to hazard the threat of war, but let us still be frank with ourselves as to what we do. Let us not call wrong right, as we have already called Germany's destruction of a weaker neighbour by smoother words than it deserved.

For that would be the last surrender—that of honest speech, even before Hitler's orders for its restriction have reached our ears.

CHAPTER XXX.

THE RESULTS OF
ABANDONING CZECHOSLOVAKIA

It is often difficult to visualise the effect of a single change upon its environment in advance of the event, but it may be of vital consequence to do so accurately.

It was impossible to impress even normally intelligent people with the certain consequences of a German entrance into Czechoslovakia until the catastrophe had occurred. They visualised it as the return of a small German minority to the integrity of a Fatherland from which they had been nefariously exiled, and though German manners might be bad and their methods of approaching the problem not quite what we would have liked them to be, the matter was still one in which it did not much concern us to interfere, even if it should not be regarded with friendly eyes.

In the same way, the return to Germany of the colonies which she seized towards the close of the last century and lost thirty years later, is vaguely visualised as an act of goodwill, good-humour, "appeasement," or even justice, without detailed consideration of what it would involve, or imaginative foresight of how we should be placed on the next day.

The episode of Czechoslovakia is at an end, and its price has been largely paid. It was France's dishonour rather than ours, for it was she who had pledged herself to that country's defence. It was she who had advised the fortification of frontiers which she afterwards pressed her ally to abandon without even receiving monetary compensation for the guns she must leave in the hands of her contemptuous foe.

We may be said to have done no more than to have looked down a path of dishonour with tempted eyes where France has gone far ahead. For it is a fact that we mobilised our fleet, and had France been true to her own pledge, we should have gone, however reluctantly, into a war which was not primarily ours.

The Price of "Peace"

All of which is common knowledge now, and need not be recalled except for the lesson that may lie in the fact that France, whose honour was the more darkly soiled, is the one who comes out with the far heavier loss. Six months ago she had strong alliances in Eastern Europe. Where are they now? She had given pledges on which weaker nations relied. What would her word be worth in the Near East now, from Latvia to Greece?

Poland—a country with a historic habit of choosing the wrong side, which has destroyed her before, and may again—deserted her instantly, though it is an easy prophecy that she will soon be knocking again at what may prove to be a closed door. The Russian alliance, always of dubious value, is more unreliable now than it was before.

Czechoslovakia, which might have engaged thirty German divisions for many weeks, even if it had done no better than that, is a lost friend. Her aeroplanes might have been less than sufficient for her own defence, but, at the least, they would have brought many of those of Germany down. The guns that pointed across the German frontier from those fortifications which French engineers and Czech labour had made so strong, have been moved now—thirteen hundred of them, it is said—to point from the German frontiers, not against Czechoslovakia, which has become negligible, but against the frontiers of France herself.

The Price France Paid

That was the Munich price which France paid because she dare not face the threat (or the bluff) of war. She bought, at a great price, something which we call peace for lack of a more accurate word.

Our Price Would Be?

What, we have to ask ourselves, is what price would be ours to pay if we should go by the same road, giving, for nominal peace, lands which are not ours except as being held in a high trust for those who occupy them, and are too weak for their own defence?—who have supposed for the last twenty years that they could safely "Take shelter underneath our shield."

It might be no less than the disintegration of the British Commonwealth, which, with all its faults and imperfections, is the most successful experiment in political, social, and international freedoms of which history has record.

It would break up because it would have proved incompetent or unwilling to defend those whom it had admitted to its peaceful fold.

Two Essential Conditions

The existence of the British Commonwealth of Allied Nations depends upon two essential conditions: that the possibility of internecine warfare has been put away, and that it may be strong enough to defend itself from outer foes.

The first of these conditions is well established, as is also that of permanent peace with the United States, and it is in this direction, and not in that of conciliating nations which still make war their god, that the best hope of the world's peace lies.

But the second condition is equally basic.

The Probable Consequences of Surrender

A month might not elapse after the Nazi landing at Dar es Salaam, and we might still be discussing, so far as discussion would be allowed, the increase in the German fleet which her new colonies would make so urgently necessary, before Kenya would have reluctantly realised that the goodwill of Berlin had become more important than that of London to her. And Cape Town might not be long in realising, if not exactly the same thing, at least that the landing of Nazi troops in South-West Africa implied that she must make herself strong for her separate defence, or her liberties would not much longer survive.

Australia, being told that Great Britain would not support her in the retention of New Guinea, might evacuate it without resistance, and New Zealand might abandon Samoa with the same docility. For what else could they do? But what would their thoughts—what would their positions—be on the next day?

How would they face the menace of Japan, with the British name eclipsed in the East, and with Germany also about their door?

Canada, faced by the same threat—for what is it but the prestige of the British name which has saved its western territories from Japanese penetration?—would turn her eyes to the United States for help in a common cause.

Great Britain herself, isolated and discredited, her trade shrinking as the dictator countries tightened their economic grip on a cowering world, her population continuing to diminish (for it is certain that a government which had surrendered without strife to an outer foe would not have spirit—which it lacks now—remaining to deal with that internal cancer), would look outward no longer to conquered seas, but only backward to a great past, and inward at its final shame.

Surely, if we are to be Carthage to Rome, which is not yet clear, we can make a better ending than that!

It may seem that we are far above such an abyss. But it is certain that we had begun to slip, and it is a descent which must be arrested, if at all, at the top of the slope.

CHAPTER XXXI.

Hitler's Contempt

We have Hitler's contempt today, to which we cannot reasonably object. He regards democracy and incompetence as synonymous words. He can point to reason for that, both in regard to ourselves and our allies. Have we not a government which thought gas-masks more important than guns? Did not Yugoslavia order ten destroyers from Germany because France would not exert herself to make punctual delivery, preferring her bankrupt treasury and her forty-hour week to the prosperity which only industry breeds?

Italy Crows on the Fence

Italy also crows on the fence. Signor Virginio Gayda, who has been called the mouthpiece of Mussolini, writing in the *Giornale d'Italia* (November 4, 1938), discussing the world position, and the possibility of any recalcitrance among the effete democracies, observed that there may still be some who may make trouble before they recognise their subordinate position. "But," he concluded comfortably, "Italy, Germany, and Japan can impose any solution they wish by force."

Too High a Boast

It is a kind of boasting with which we are unlikely to compete, and it is with no disposition to underestimate the power for evil of these three somewhat blustering allies that we may remark that, so far, they have done little, beyond the piling up of armaments, to justify so extreme a vaunt.

Japan's unprovoked assault upon China is not the species of military operation which demonstrates the quality of an army as opposed to one of high training and equipment; and the end is not yet.

As to Italy, we had a war with Abyssinia once ourselves. We may compare it confidently with Italy's adventures in the same region, alike in respect of its occasion, its conduct, and its consequence. And we neither had aeroplanes nor a huge mechanised army for our support, nor did we regard its success as a world-shaking event.

As to the record of Italian arms in Spain, there is no need to say much and, indeed, there is not much to say.

We do not disparage Italian valour nor the Italian nation, who may have our friendship, if they will, on most easy terms. But we may think that Signor Gayda boasts of something which is not proved.

At the same time it is necessary to observe that Hitler takes an even more truculent tone. His Weimar speech of November 6, 1938 was one prolonged violence of vituperation towards two of the four Powers of Western

Europe who, by the Munich precedent and the peace pact he signed with Mr. Chamberlain on that occasion, were to combine to smooth out the political problems which disturb the world.

It is too evident that his idea of such co-operation is that Great Britain and France shall be subordinate partners, attending to take orders, or to make humble protests, rather than to enter into discussion on equal terms.

Indeed, Hitler has been ill-manneredly frank on that point. He said a few days earlier that negotiation (and it is most probable that this question of colonies was on his mind) is not to be interpreted as compromise. It is understood in advance that he must have everything he desires, and the conferences will be no more than convenient occasions for arranging the details of the event.

Like Signor Gayda, Herr Hitler boasts that he is far stronger than we, and that force is the final court of appeal; but he expressed surprise that we should think it necessary to arm ourselves. It was as though the Munich lesson of subordination had not been completely learned!

And he warned us, both in that speech and in the more recent one of January 31, 1939, that to include Mr. Winston Churchill, Mr. Duff Cooper, or Mr. Anthony Eden in future governments would be unwise. It is a matter on which he thinks that the final vote should come from his own mouth.

Courtesy between nations is well, and it is well that their statesmen should be of good accord; but if there is to be a purging of that kind, let it be pursued equally in all lands, and the resignations of Herren Hitler, Göring, and Goebbels should head the list.

We are arming now—more or less vigorously—it having penetrated into the minds of our Inner Cabinet that they could not hope to defeat any country so long as 40,000,000 gas-masks were the main item of our military equipment—which Herr Hitler resents.

But he knows that we have no aggressive purpose. He knows that we desire peace. He knows that, if the gentlemen whose words annoy him were at the head of a British Government tomorrow, they would make no war so long as he should act in a neighbourly manner. His disquiet at our moderate armaments can only arise from a fear, not that we shall attack him, but that we should resist some indignity which he plans for a future day.

It is a warning which we shall be obtuse if we do not heed.

CHAPTER XXXII.

THE MILLIONS OF DECENT GERMANS

It would be a radical error of diagnosis to fail to recognise that there must be millions of decent Germans who desire peace for themselves and the world, and who are as antipathetic as ourselves to the brutality of the Nazi rule.

It is said, and should be as readily believed as are accounts of more sinister events, that the Berliners who picnicked in woods to which hunted Jews had fled, and in which they starved, readily shared their own sandwiches with these persecuted outcasts, though they must have done even this act of elementary humanity at some risk, knowing that scores of their fellow-citizens had been jailed for no worse offence than verbal condemnation of the cruelties inflicted upon these innocent people.

For the moment, such elements of the German nation, whether few or many, have no power, and must be disregarded when we assess the immediate dangers we have to face. But the moment does not endure; nor does Hitler's criminal authority remain precisely the same for a single hour. It must fluctuate under a thousand influences, and it should surely be the aim of every civilised government throughout the world to avoid any action which may tend to increase his prestige, or that of his intimate colleagues, and so prolong the danger of which all nations have become acutely aware.

Opportunities Lost

There have been opportunities, more than one, when we might have done much to expose or discredit him to his own nation as the force which drags them through slavery to the abyss, but we have either ignored them, or dealt with them in such a way as actually to augment, and probably to prolong his power.

Most recently the whole world has been given an opportunity, by the shameless plundering and persecution of the Jewish citizens of Germany, of expressing its indignation through the withdrawal of its accredited envoys, and has let it pass.

Had every ambassador and envoy left Berlin after delivering an identical note to the effect that he had been sent under the mistaken impression that he was being accredited to a civilised government, the truth of the event could hardly have been concealed from the German public, and its moral effect upon them might have been profound, even though the Japanese and Italian flags might still have flown over their legation buildings, to demonstrate the solidity of all peoples of Nordic blood!

But, probably from lack of imaginations, rather than wills, the opportunity of world-rebuke has gone by. Hitler, for the moment, has satisfied his treasury's desperate needs by that wholesale theft; and German citizens, looking on, may try to persuade themselves that there are excuses for what he did.

Opportunities Which We Do Not Miss

We have let that opportunity pass, but there are those of an opposite kind which we do not miss.

To give Hitler colonies—even to expose to the German public that we are paltering with the idea—might be to give him further years of assured and augmented power.

Each objective he is allowed to gain increases his most dangerous arrogance, and makes his otherwise precarious position in Germany more secure. Each time that he and his associates appear likely to bankrupt their popularity, we allow them fresh counters with which to play the infernal game.

A War to Protect Our Peace

We have allowed ourselves to be forced into a position where, however reluctantly, we may be driven to fight; and, if we are, we shall not again talk of a war to end war, which is absurd, but of a war to protect our peace, which is precisely what it will be. For it is the peace of the British Commonwealth of Nations, the peace of freedom in thought and speech, which we should defend, and which is worth defending, even at a great cost.

Mr. Malcolm MacDonald, in a recent message to the National Liberal candidate at Doncaster (November 12, 1938), appeared to think that it cannot be saved, or perhaps we should say is not worth saving, being too weak to endure the hard ordeal of war. He said:

What Mr. Malcolm MacDonald Thinks of Democracy

There are those who urge that we should cease to strive for peace, and that war is inevitable if democracy is to be saved. Those who advocate this course have little foresight. Whoever won another war, democracy would certainly be counted among the casualties. In the anarchy of war and its aftermath, people would turn to more facile and desperate forms of government. If there be a long period of peace I believe that liberty will gradually extend its sway again; if war came, it would be doomed.

Well, if that be so, it is a case of *Heil, Hitler!*—for he has shown us the better way. If democracy can only exist by his forbearing permission, we may well look round for a more secure foundation on which to build.

But while continuing to urge that we should *not* cease to strive for peace, though recognising that the shadow of war grows darker with every week, and believing that, if the position were faced more boldly, there would be better hope (though still not much) that it would withdraw, it is still possible to think Mr. MacDonald's faith in "democracy"—by which, however, we may not mean quite the same thing—to be weaker than it deserves.

The Peril We Have to Face

In any case, we shall not alter facts by objecting to recognise that we are facing a world-peril of the first magnitude, nor that it is one that has a deeper root than the character and ambitions of Adolf Hitler, or the terms of the Versailles Treaty—for were there not the same instincts, the same intentions, even the same methods, in the policies and practices of the old German Empire, and in those of the Prussian kingdom from which it came?

The wars which Bismarck deliberately provoked seventy or eighty years ago were the first sparks of a kindling fire which now threatens to consume the world.

We may have no right—and no disposition—to interfere with the internal economy of another state or its choice of rulers, so long as they do not directly endanger ourselves, but when the author of such a book as M*ein Kampf*—even as it is expurgated for the delusion of English readers—becomes the supreme head of eighty million people, and sacrifices all other interests to arm and discipline them for war, it is a position in which we may well be roused to assert and protect ourselves; for he has made it clear that he will not long be placated by gifts or by cringing words; nor can we pay such tribute to him and retain the respect of other hostile elements in a watchful world.

CHAPTER XXXIII.

THE ITALIAN CLAIMS UPON FRANCE

It was only as this book was being finally revised for the press that the Italian claim for French territorial surrenders became blatantly audible.

In advance of that outcry, it had seemed inexpedient to suggest a *casus belli* which had not become articulate in the world's ears, beyond the brief allusion to Tunisia (see Chapter XXV), the meaning of which would be plain enough to those who already knew.

But there can no longer be occasion for any reticence. Demands have been made upon France, in a manner of deliberate insolence, for territorial concessions of an intolerable character, which those who still strive and hope for the preservation of peace argue may not be literally meant. They suggest that the surrender of Djibouti, with some adjustment of Suez Canal tolls, and some administrative changes in Tunisia, may be sufficient to satisfy the Italian appetite, and that France may be disposed even to such terms as those, if she can obtain the withdrawal of the Italian forces from Spain by no other means.

Those who judge France in that way may be widely wrong. But even if that be contemplated as a possible settlement, it remains difficult to suppose that Italy would look on it in the same way. For such proposals would most naturally have been made through the ordinary diplomatic channels, and with a courtesy which would have made them less difficult to discuss.

If, however, the demands which have been put forward are to be taken literally, and are intended, under sufficiently favourable circumstances, to be pushed to the decision of war, it is easy to see that nothing would be gained by any courtesy of presentation, they being so destitute of moderation or equity that they could be granted, if at all, only in a spirit of abject fear.

Such surrenders are rarely asked, except from a beaten foe, and they appear to spring from a conviction that France, having abandoned Czechoslovakia, will accept whatever further humiliations may be required rather than appeal to the decision of arms.

Does This Concern Us?

It may be superficially argued that these demands do not directly concern ourselves, and still less the subject with which we are dealing; but this is not so.

The position is that Britain and France, acting in alliance, have already suffered diplomatic defeats of the gravest character, and the opinion is influentially held in consequence, both in Germany and Italy, that either France or ourselves will make almost any sacrifice rather than face the hazardous horrors of European conflict.

They are confident that they can obtain more than they have yet got, the only doubt being how much.

That is while Britain and France show a united front. To separate the two—to induce either to yield—would, they consider, remove the last possibility of resistance; and there would be nothing more to be done but to look round the larders of the democracies, and select their meals.

In this conclusion they may be wrong, on more points than one. The British Empire, with its existence at stake, might, as Earl Baldwin has truly said, fight with a unity and determination it has never previously known, even though it should find itself faced by a world in arms.

It faced a comparable position in the early years of last century, to which Mr. Neville Chamberlain, visualising the possibility that it might recur, alluded in the noblest passage of his Birmingham speech.

Our position then was similar to what it would now be if Germany should have subdued France; and at that time the United States were not of a friendly temper. Yet Austerlitz was balanced by Trafalgar, and in the end we won through.

So it may be again. It is a danger we should not seek, yet which may be hard to avoid.

The circulation of the Berlin-Rome axis may be that if, at the same time, Germany shall press for colonial, and Italy shall press France for territorial, concessions, separately, but on parallel lines, one or other (if not both) will give way. And if either should falter, they may believe, rightly or wrongly, that both will fall.

France, having surrendered Tunisia and Djibouti for her own peace, would not readily fight to save Tanganyika for us. Or if we can be bullied or cajoled into handing back the ex-German colonies, we shall be ill-disposed to fight to save Djibouti for France on the next day.

The preservation of peace in Europe depends upon many incalculable factors. Some of us may think it to be, at the best, no more than a slender hope; others accept Herr Hitler's assurances in a more sanguine spirit. But we are all agreed that it is the supreme issue of our time, and whatever the prospect be must finally depend upon the replies which both Great Britain and France give to these monstrous claims being so worded that those who have made them will realise that there is no more to be had, unless it be by the path of disarmament and goodwill, or at the cost of most bitter war.

Three Choices

With or without the French alliance, we have three choices before us. We may meet these colonial claims with a firm and unequivocal negative, with a debatable possibility of war resulting. We may surrender to German demands, and so gain some period of shamed, precarious peace. Or we may adopt an attitude of timid compromise, hesitating either to yield or deny, which is the way of war, certain and soon.

For the German demand is not of a casual character. It has been the subject of prolonged agitation in Germany, and of elaborately organised propaganda in this country and in the threatened colonies for more than three years past, which has been intensified during recent months.

Every week the hopes of the German people are more highly raised upon a subject which we may ignore, but they are not allowed to forget; every week their expectations are more inflamed. The Reich Colonial League, the members of which are pledged to work for the return of the lost territories, was founded in 1935. It has branches throughout Germany which are controlled from Berlin, and which conduct an incessant propaganda, representing the colonies as still being parts of the Fatherland, only temporarily held apart, which their Führer has pledged himself to regain, as he will be sure and speedy to do.

Consistently with this expectation, the German Foreign Office is refusing passports to Jews, even when under sentence of expulsion, if their final destination be given as South-West Africa or Tanganyika, on the ground that they will not tolerate their presence in German colonies.

The League publishes a *Year Book*. The 1939 edition assumes and asserts that England will surrender promptly to German demands.

"The day will come," Herr Karlowa (a Nazi politician on the foreign staff of Hitler's personal deputy, Rudolf Hess) confidently asserts, "when the Führer, after peaceful discussions with the other colonial Powers, will call on the German youth to commence its march into the colonies."

The propaganda value of this *Year Book* may be no less in its own country because it asserts many things— such as the "attitude of race pollution" alleged to be adopted by ourselves toward native peoples; the "vanished trust of the coloured peoples in the leadership of the white races" which Germany is to restore; or the superior security which the native African will enjoy under the protection of the National Socialist Labour Front—which appear fantastic to us.

A prominent article in the *Zwölf-Uhr Blatt* (February 1, 1939), purporting to include quotations urging the surrender of colonies from "three British politicians," was exposed in the London Press as particularly impudent mendacity. The only accurate quotation which it contained was some observations from the pen of Professor Dawson.

But its exposure will not come under German eyes, and the cumulative effect of such methods, supported, as they are, by an insidious propaganda which finds its way, through whatever channels, into some British newspapers, and is then reproduced in Germany—as representing authoritative British opinion—may be very great.

The demand for more than the return of the conquered colonies which is most recently being made—this is, for a surrender of a proportion of the British Empire which would leave the colonial possessions of Great Britain and Germany in the ratios of their home populations—may sound too crazy for serious consideration. But it remains sufficiently serious fact that the German Colonial League should have been officially instructed to commence to agitate for that solution.

It will be noticed that the procedure is precisely that which was practised against Austria and Czechoslovakia—that of the constantly increasing demand, so that all concessions must lag behind.

Against such methods, and with such examples to warn us, we shall do well to let it be known at once, in the clearest words, that we shall hold our frontiers intact, rather than fall back upon weaker lines.

ABOUT THE AUTHOR

SYDNEY FOWLER WRIGHT (1874-1965) penned over seventy volumes of science fiction, fantasy, classic mysteries, historical novels, poetry, and non-fiction, many of them being published by the Borgo Press Imprint of Wildside Press.

www.ingramcontent.com/pod-product-compliance
Lightning Source LLC
Chambersburg PA
CBHW030934090426
42737CB00007B/425